Read, Sing, and Play Along!

Gross and Annoying Songs

School Specialty Publishing

Columbus, Ohio

Send all inquiries to:
School Specialty Publishing
8720 Orion Place
Columbus, Ohio 43240-2111

ISBN 0-7696-4317-5

1 2 3 4 5 6 7 8 9 10 WAF 10 09 08 07 06

Table of Contents

Wild and Wacky Experiments

Introduction

Would you like to bend bones in your bare hands or change a foul-smelling liquid from putrid purple to putrescent pink with a drop of acid? If these activities sound like your cup of goo, this collection of slippery, slimy, freaky, and fun experiments is for you. They are guaranteed to offend the senses!

Most of the experiments can be performed in a small amount of space with ingredients you probably have around the house. Before you begin, read these important safety procedures!

- Always work with an adult.
- Wash your hands before and after each experiment.
- Read the instructions all they way through before starting any experiment.
- If you need to use heat or sharp objects in the test, be sure to ask an adult to give you a hand.
- Never taste anything unless the instructions specifically say it is okay.
- Clean up everything when you are finished.

Ready to begin? If you have a strong stomach, you'll love doing these experiments!

Magic Mud

Some substances don't dissolve in water; instead, they do something very interesting. Try the experiment below to create magic mud.

Materials

- 4-ounce bottle of white glue
- $1\frac{1}{2}$ cups distilled water
- two medium glass bowls
- two spoons
- 1 teaspoon borax powder

Directions

❶ Mix the entire bottle of glue and $\frac{1}{2}$ cup distilled water in one bowl. Stir with a spoon.

❷ Pour 1 cup distilled water and 1 teaspoon borax powder into the second bowl. Stir well with the second spoon.

❸ Pour the glue mixture into the borax mixture and stir until you have a thick blob.

4 Lift the mixture out of the bowl and knead it with your hands until it feels like dough. Try ripping it, pulling it apart slowly, and even bouncing it.

How did this work?

The white glue is made up of polymers that become suspended in water. Before you mix the glue with anything else, these polymers tend to slide over each other. Adding borax to the glue causes the polymers to stop moving and form a sort of meshwork instead. The result is a concentrated suspension—liquid water with lots of tiny solid particles (in this case, the polymers) suspended in it. The solid particles do not fit into the spaces between the water molecules, so they can't dissolve in the liquid.

Them Bones!

Your friends and family will be amazed when they see you tying a bone in knots.

Materials

- drumstick or wishbone from a chicken
- scrub brush
- glass jar with a lid, large enough to hold the bone
- white vinegar

Directions

❶ After a nice chicken dinner, save the bone you want to use for your experiment. With the scrub brush, carefully clean all the meat and gristle from the bone and allow it to dry for a few hours.

❷ Fill the jar with vinegar, drop the bone in, and put on the lid. Leave the jar undisturbed for 3 days.

③ Remove the bone from the vinegar and rinse it with water. It should be soft and rubbery enough to tie in a knot. If it isn't, prepare a fresh jar of vinegar and leave the bone in it for another day or two.

How did this work?

Two main elements make up bone. Collagen is a protein that makes bones strong and resilient. Without it, they become very brittle. Apatite is a mineral that makes bones hard. The vinegar is a weak acid that dissolves the apatite in the bone but leaves behind the rubbery collagen.

Fun Fact
The strongest bone in the human body is the femur, or thigh bone. It can support more weight than a rod of equal size made of solid steel.

Naked Egg

Have you ever peeled an egg . . . a raw egg, that is? There's a delightfully slimy surprise inside.

Materials

- raw egg
- glass jar with lid
- white vinegar

Directions

❶ Put the egg in the jar, being very careful not to crack the shell.

❷ Fill the jar with enough vinegar to completely cover the egg. Put on the lid and leave the jar undisturbed for about 3 days.

❸ If you check once in a while, you'll see lots of tiny bubbles on the eggshell. When few bubbles are left and the shell is dissolved, very gently pour the vinegar out over the sink so you can catch the egg. Hold it very carefully and observe. It feels soft and slippery. Don't squeeze it or the egg will break.

❹ Hold it up to a light. You can easily see the yolk inside. If you want to save the egg for a while, refill the jar with water, slip the egg in, and replace the lid. It will keep well in the refrigerator for a few days.

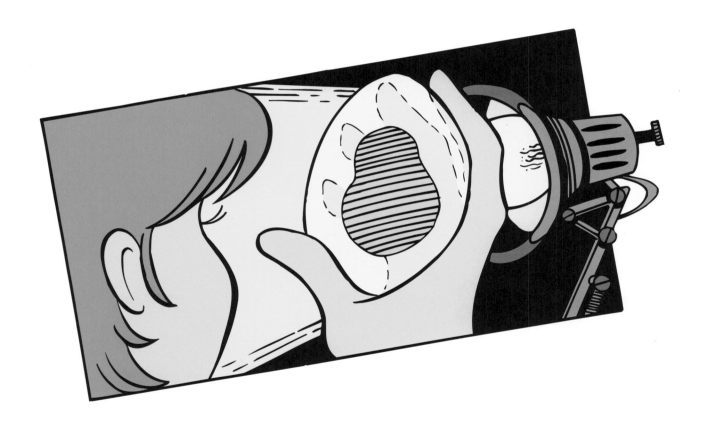

How did this work?

The eggshell is made up of a material called *calcium carbonate*. The vinegar reacts with the shell, dissolving it and producing tiny bubbles of carbon dioxide gas. Just inside the egg is a thin membrane that does not react to the vinegar. The membrane keeps the egg intact. Within is the yolk, which is meant to be the food supply for a developing embryo. This is surrounded by the egg white, or albumen, which helps cushion the embryo.

Fun Fact

If you store your shell-less egg in water, it will swell because of osmosis. Water moves through the egg membrane, but the molecules that make up the goopy material inside the egg are too big to go the other way. That's called semipermeability.

To see the opposite reaction, place the shell-less, raw egg in a jar of sticky corn syrup. There is more water in the egg than in the corn syrup, so the water molecules will leave the egg. The egg will shrivel into a gooey, yucky mess . . . er, mass.

Morbid Bleeding Blobs

These drippy spheres are guaranteed to make you gasp. What makes them bob? How do they bleed?

Materials

- empty baby-food jar
- rubbing alcohol
- water
- measuring spoons
- mixing spoon
- vegetable oil
- small paper cup
- eyedropper
- red food coloring
- paper towels

Directions

❶ Fill the jar halfway with rubbing alcohol. Add 5 teaspoons of water. Stir the mixture with a spoon, then set the jar aside and wait for the liquid to stop moving.

❷ Meanwhile, place 4 teaspoons of vegetable oil into the paper cup. Add 2 drops of red food coloring, then use the eyedropper to quickly stir the food coloring into the oil. The food coloring stays separated from the oil in tiny balls. Keep mixing and the oil, as it turns blood-red, will look like it blends completely with the food coloring.

❸ Fill the eyedropper with the food coloring and oil mixture. Carefully lower the eyedropper into the jar of alcohol and water solution and place the tip just below the surface. Squeeze the end of the dropper to release a blob of colored oil. Take the eyedropper out of the jar and squeeze out the extra oil onto a paper towel. Refill the eyedropper with more colored oil and repeat the process until you have three or four blobs in the jar.

❹ Watch the result. Your goal is to have the blobs floating in the middle of the jar. But your blood-red blobs will probably do one of two things:

- They will sink. (If they settle at the bottom of the jar, you can add more water, a teaspoon at a time, to make the blobs rise.)

- They will float. (If they rise to the top, you can add more alcohol, a teaspoon at a time, to make the blobs sink.)

Once in a great while, one kid in about 8 million will mix the alcohol and water perfectly on the first try, making the red blobs settle in the middle of the jar. For the rest of you, as you patiently add water or alcohol, teaspoon by teaspoon, watch this process from the side of the jar. Don't place your face near the top of the jar—it puts you in contact with harmful fumes.

❺ When the blobs are in position, put the lid back on the jar. Peer carefully at the blobs. How do they stay where they are? Why do they look like they're bleeding?

Important! *Once you've finished admiring your bleeding blobs, immediately pour the liquid down the sink, then run tap water for a minute or two. Do not leave it standing around where anyone, especially small children, can get to it. Rubbing alcohol is highly* **toxic** *if swallowed.*

How did this work?

There are a couple of things going on in this experiment. The first is a demonstration of **density**, the ratio of weight to **volume** in an object or substance. The oil-based blobs bob in the middle of the jar because the alcohol and water mixture is lighter than water yet heavier than alcohol. In a perfectly mixed **solution**, the blobs are somewhere in between, density-wise—they neither sink to the bottom nor float to the top of the jar.

This experiment is also an example of **immiscible liquids**, or liquids that do not mix together. The oil stays in a round blob because it won't mix with water or alcohol. The blob "bleeds" because the food coloring mixes better with water and alcohol than it does with oil, making food coloring and oil immiscible liquids, too.

Fun Fact

There is an old saying that oil and water do not mix. In science lingo, they are immiscible liquids, and there have been many tragic examples of this in the earth's oceans. Anyone who has seen or smelled an oil slick knows just how disgusting it can be. Oil from shipping accidents floats on top of ocean water and eventually makes its way toward the shore, where it leaves an ugly black sludge. To clean up an oil slick, some countries use a chemical spray that makes the oil sink deeper in the water, keeping it away from shore. Others clean up an oil slick by spraying detergent, which breaks up the oil into smaller particles that are then more readily broken up by ocean microorganisms.

The See-Through Hand

You can't always believe what you see. Sometimes your eyes play tricks on you. These are known as optical illusions.

Materials

- sheet of construction paper
- tape

Directions

❶ Roll the paper into a tube big enough to look through comfortably with one eye. Tape the paper so that it will not unravel.

❷ Look through the tube with your right eye. Keep your left eye open and look straight ahead. Place your left hand against the far end of the tube, with the palm facing you. Move your hand slowly a few inches from the end of the tube. Stare straight ahead as you do this, not at your hand. What do you see?

How did this work?

Both of your eyes face forward, so your field of vision overlaps. This is called binocular vision. The brain tries to blend what each eye sees into one image. In this case, the left eye sees the hand and the right eye sees the hole. The brain perceives this as a hand with a hole in it.

Another Fun Optical Illusion

Hold your index fingers in front of your eyes. Point your fingers at each other but leave an inch-wide gap between them. Keep both eyes open. After a minute you will see a tiny "fingertip" in between your real fingers.

Criss-Cross

Your brain is your center of intelligence. But even the brain can be fooled sometimes.

Materials

- one marble

Directions

1. Place the marble on a flat surface.

2. Cross your middle and index fingers.

3. Close your eyes and gently roll the marble back and forth. Be sure that you touch the marble with the tips of both fingers. What do you feel?

How did this work?

You understand the world through your senses. The nerve endings in your fingertips send messages to your brain. By crossing your fingers, you confuse your brain, and it interprets the feeling as two marbles rather than one.

Fun With Friends

Ask a friend to close his or her eyes and cross his or her fingers. Place five or six marbles on a small, flat plate. Ask your friend to roll them around and try to figure out how many marbles there are.

What a Kick!

Believe it or not, what your feet are doing can have an effect on your ability to write!

Materials

- straight-backed chair
- table
- pencil and paper
- an observer

Directions

❶ Sit up straight in the chair, near enough to the table to write. Using the pencil and paper, write the sentence *A quick black cat jumped over the brick wall.*

❷ Lift your right leg up off the floor and begin to turn it in wide circles from right to left.

❸ Try to write the sentence again while moving your leg. Ask your observer to be sure that your leg keeps going in a circular pattern. Can you write the sentence as easily as you did the first time?

How did this work?

Your actions are governed by your brain. It takes concentration to move your leg in a circular motion and to write a sentence. When you focus on one, you lose control of the other. It is possible to do both at the same time, but it takes a lot of practice.

Here Comes the Sludge

Whip up some strange behavior in a bowl. What does it do? Find out . . . if you have the nerve.

Materials

- mixing spoon
- 4-ounce bottle of white glue
- measuring cups
- 1 pint distilled water
- 2 medium-sized glass bowls
- food coloring, any color, or mix up a particularly gross yellow-green
- 1 teaspoon borax powder

Directions

❶ With a spoon, mix the contents of the bottle of glue and ½ cup distilled water in one bowl. Add 5 drops of food coloring and stir well.

❷ Pour 1 cup of distilled water and the borax powder in the second bowl. Stir well.

❸ Pour the glue mixture into the borax mixture and keep stirring until you have a thick glob. Lift it out of the bowl and knead the mixture until it feels like dough. The behavior of the sludge depends on what you do to it, so get creative! Rip the sludge in two. Find out what happens when you pull it slowly. Will it bounce?

How did this work?

This is another slippery, slimy example of a non-Newtonian fluid. It is a concentrated suspension. That means it's a liquid with lots of tiny, solid particles suspended in it. The solid particles do not dissolve in the liquid. In fact, they can be removed by passing the liquid through a filter. You can try this yourself using a pint-sized glass jar and a number four coffee filter. Simply place the filter in the top of the jar and slowly pour the liquid into it. The solid material left behind in the filter is called a residue.

Along Came a Spider

Little Miss Muffet wasn't crazy about spiders, but she loved curds and whey. Here's how to whip up a batch for yourself!

Materials

- 1 quart skim milk (1%, 2%, and whole milk also work)
- saucepan
- mixing spoon
- 2 tablespoons lemon juice
- colander or sieve
- cheesecloth

Directions

❶ Pour the milk into the saucepan. With an adult's help, stir constantly over medium heat, bringing it to a slow boil. Keep a close watch on it because milk can boil over quite suddenly.

❷ Have your adult helper remove the pan from the heat and stir in the lemon juice.

❸ Return the pan to the heat and stir the milky mixture until you see lumps. Turn off the heat and let the milk cool to room temperature.

4 Line the colander or sieve with cheesecloth and put it in the sink. Pour the milk through the colander. The pale fluid running down the drain is called whey. The lumps left behind in the colander are the curds, a simplified version of cottage cheese! It is certainly safe to eat, though you may not find it very tasty.

How did this work?

When a water-soluble protein, such as that in milk, is heated to a certain temperature, or acid is added, it becomes denatured. (In this experiment both heat and acid are used.) "Denatured" means a change takes place and the protein will no longer remain dissolved in a fluid. It forms clumps, or curds. The acid in the lemon juice causes such a chemical reaction when it comes in contact with protein in the milk. The result is curds and whey. The clumping reaction demonstrates protein coagulation. This is the process used to make cheese, a valuable source of protein in the human diet.

Fun Fact

One legend maintains that the first cheese was made by accident. Supposedly an Arabian merchant filled a pouch with milk, then after riding through the desert all day he found that the milk had separated into curds and whey. It was the heat and a substance in the lining of the pouch that caused this reaction. The substance is called rennet, and it is an enzyme, a protein that helps a chemical reaction take place. Like lemon juice, rennet contributes to the milk-curdling reaction in milk. The pouch, by the way, was made out of a sheep's stomach.

Slime Time

Is it a solid or a liquid? This slippery, slimy ooze has a split personality.

Materials

- 1 cup cornstarch
- mixing bowl
- water
- measuring spoons
- mixing spoon

Directions

❶ Put the cornstarch in the bowl. Add water by the teaspoonful and stir. Keep adding teaspoons of water until the mixture is fluid but very hard to stir. It should have the consistency of thick mud.

❷ Reach in and pick up a handful of the gooey fluid. Don't be squeamish— you have to move fast for this to work. Quickly roll the glop between your hands. It will become a firm ball.

❸ Hold your hands over the bowl and stop rolling. The ball becomes fluid again and slippery slime drips through your fingers.

How did this work?

Your slime is an example of a non-Newtonian fluid. Fluids have a property called viscosity, or resistance to flow. The British scientist Sir Isaac Newton (1642–1727) is best known for his theories about light, gravity, and motion. He said that the viscosity of a fluid, such as water, can be changed only by raising or lowering its temperature. Sometimes in science you'll find an exception to a rule, and non-Newtonian fluids are the exception to Sir Isaac's rule on viscosity. Non-Newtonian fluids can be changed by temperature or, as shown in this experiment, by applying force. Putting pressure on the slippery slime by rubbing it between your hands makes it resistant to flowing.

Fun Fact

Believe it or not, glass is not a solid but rather a very viscous liquid. Adding heat will cause glass to flow. Non-Newtonian fluids, like glass, may also change over time. If you are lucky enough to live near a very old building that has the original glass in its windows, check closely. You may find that the panes are a tiny bit thicker at the bottom. That is because the glass has flowed ever so slightly downward over many years.

Demented Dessert

In an old movie called **The Blob,** *a creature that looked a lot like an oversized lump of gelatin gobbled up a bellyful of townsfolk. Usually it's the other way around— flavored gelatin is a great dessert that kids can really sink their teeth into. It also makes a gooey, oozy example of a rather unusual substance. Try this experiment, then feel free to eat the evidence.*

Materials

- 1 cup apple juice
- saucepan
- small glass bowl (Pyrex® is recommended)
- 1 packet unflavored gelatin
- mixing spoon
- butter knife
- microwave-safe plate

Directions

❶ Pour the cup of apple juice into the pan and warm it over medium heat until it comes to a boil. Ask an adult to remove the juice from the heat and pour it into a glass bowl.

❷ Sprinkle in the unflavored gelatin. Stir until the powder dissolves, and refrigerate for several hours.

❸ Once the gelatin has set completely, remove it from the bowl in one piece. To do this, place the bowl in warm water for 2 minutes. Then run a butter knife around the edge of the gelatin. Slide the gelatin carefully onto a microwave-safe plate.

❹ Now place the wiggly gelatin in a microwave on medium power for about 30 seconds, then check it. (If you don't have a microwave, you can use an oven heated on its lowest setting. You'll need to substitute an oven-safe plate for a microwave-safe plate.) You should see that the juice has been released and the slippery ooze is seeping across the plate. If your microwave has a clear door, you can even watch as the gelatin begins to "sweat."

Read, Sing, and Play Along! Gross and Annoying Songs

How did this work?

Gelatin dessert is a substance known as a *colloid*. A colloid is made up of very tiny particles, called the *solute*, in a liquid, called the *solvent*. If the solute is solid and the solvent is liquid, then the colloid is known as a *sol* (such as milk and glue). If the solute and the solvent are both liquid, the colloid is called an emulsion (such as mayonnaise).

In this experiment, the colloid is called a *gel*. The solid part is the powdered gelatin— a protein that forms a kind of mesh. When mixed with hot water (or in this case, hot apple juice), gelatin granules absorb the liquid and swell, then melt. As the solution cools and is chilled, the liquid is trapped within the mesh network. The network a colloid forms is broken down by heat. When you put your gelatin in the microwave, the fluid was released because the network trapping it was no longer in place.

> **Fun Fact**
> *Gelatin is a substance that can be made by boiling animal cartilage, hides, skin, and bone in water, then letting the result cool until it sets into a gel.*

Groaning Glass

These grating sound effects can set your teeth on edge. Try it with glasses of different sizes, and you can start your own creepy chorus.

Materials

- stem wineglass (the thinner the glass the better)
- dishwashing liquid
- water
- dishtowel
- white vinegar
- small bowl

Directions

❶ Wash the glass and your hands in warm, soapy water to get rid of any grease or oil. Dry thoroughly.

❷ Holding it by the stem, place the squeaky-clean glass on a flat surface. Pour a little vinegar into the bowl (you won't need more than $\frac{1}{4}$ cup) and dip the index finger of your free hand in the vinegar.

❸ Holding the glass at its base, rub your wet finger around the rim of the glass until you hear a high-pitched whine.

How did this work?

Washing everything well and using vinegar rids the glass and your finger of any oil or **lubricant**. As you rub, you create **friction** between the rim of the glass and your finger. Friction is the resistance to motion between two surfaces moving across each other. This resistance causes the glass and surrounding air to vibrate, which you hear as a whining sound. The pitch of the sound is determined by the frequency or number of vibrations per second. The higher the frequency, the higher the pitch.

Fun Fact
The friction between your finger and the glass results in the sound you hear in this experiment. Another product of friction is heat. To feel heat from friction, try rubbing your dry hands together very fast. Do they warm up?

Which Way Worms

Like all living things, worms have ways to sense the world around them. Try this test of a worm's ability to detect odors.

Remember: The worms are your partners in this experiment and should never be harmed.

Materials

- paper towel
- water
- earthworms
- tweezers
- cotton balls
- nail polish remover

Directions

❶ Dampen a paper towel with water and place some earthworms on it to crawl around.

❷ Use the tweezers to drench a cotton ball in nail polish remover and put it near but not touching a worm's head. The end closest to the wide band on a worm's body is the head.

❸ Observe the direction in which the worm crawls. Be careful not to actually touch any of the worms. Release the worms into their natural environment when the experiment is over.

How did this work?

Even though you don't touch the worm, it moves away from the cotton ball. An earthworm doesn't have a nose. What it does have is a nerve cord that extends the length of its body, and masses of nerve tissue in each segment. This enables it to detect an unpleasant odor and change its direction.

More Fun With Worms

Will a worm be attracted to some odors and repulsed by others? Try using different scents such as vanilla, squashed banana, and bleach.

Maggot Magic

Does rotting meat turn into maggots? If rotting meat is left outside in hot weather, newly hatched flies, called maggots, soon appear in the meat. The wormlike maggots eventually grow into adult flies. The appearance of maggots in rotting meat led some ancient people to believe that rotting meat turns into maggots.

Materials

- two plastic cups
- hole punch
- scissors
- string
- two small pieces of raw meat
- small piece of cloth
- rubber band

Directions

❶ Get two plastic cups. Use a hole punch to make two holes near the rim of each cup, one on each side.

❷ Use the scissors to cut four pieces of string, each about 3 feet long. Tie the ends of the strings to the holes in the cups, one string per hole.

❸ Put a small piece of raw meat in each cup.

❹ Leave one cup uncovered. Cover the top of the other cup with a small piece of cloth. Fasten the cloth tightly with a rubber band. Put tape over the string holes in this cup, so that insects can't get in.

❺ Find a tree with a high, long branch. Ask an adult to help you tie both cups to the tree branch, high enough to be out of reach of dogs, cats, and other animals.

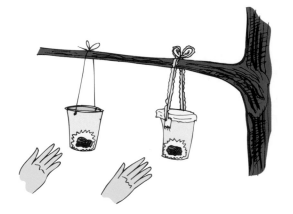

6 Ask an adult to help you smear a thick layer of petroleum jelly down the length of each string, to keep out ants.

7 Look in the cups every day until you see maggots. Where are the maggots?

How did this work?

Maggots only appeared in the uncovered cup. Flies are attracted to rotting meat, where they lay eggs. However, the flies were able to reach only the meat in the uncovered cup. The fly eggs in the uncovered cup hatched into maggots. This experiment proves that fly eggs, not rotting meat, give rise to maggots. A similar experiment was done over 300 years ago by an Italian scientist named Francesco Redi, who proved that living things don't "hatch" from nonliving substances.

More Fun With a Cup

Grow a fruit fungus. Make two holes in a plastic cup and tie strings to the holes, as described above. Place a slice of banana in the cup. Cover the top of the cup with a small piece of cloth, and fasten the cloth tightly with a rubber band. Put tape over the string holes in the cup. Tie the cup to a tree branch, out of reach of animals. Smear petroleum jelly down the length of the strings, to keep out ants. Check the banana slice after a week or two. Is something growing on the banana?

Foul Fruit

Imagine this: You have your taste buds all ready for a yummy apple. You open wide, take a big bite, and . . . disgusting! You get a mouthful of brown, mealy pulp. In this experiment, you will speed up the process of fresh, crisp fruit turning to mush.

Materials

- knife
- ripe apple or banana
- 2 small bowls
- lemon juice
- mixing spoon

Directions

❶ With an adult's help, peel the fruit and cut it into small pieces. Put half in one bowl and set it aside.

❷ Put the other half of the fruit in the second bowl, add the lemon juice, and toss with a spoon until the fruit is coated.

❸ After about 30 minutes, check the fruit in each bowl. The bare fruit should be starting to turn brown. The fruit with the lemon juice should look much fresher.

❹ Leave the fruit undisturbed for 2 more hours, then check again. By this time the bare

fruit should be quite brown. If you want to up the grossness quotient of this experiment, let the untreated fruit remain out in the bowl for several days and observe the changes it goes through.

How did this work?

Chemicals in the fruit, called **aldehydes**, combine with oxygen in the air causing a **chemical reaction**. A chemical reaction is a change that takes place when two or more substances interact. Here, the aldehydes in the fruit mix with oxygen, turning the bare fruit sickly brown. After several hours it begins to get mushy. The fruit coated with the lemon juice will also turn brown, but much more slowly, because lemon juice is a weak **acid** that delays the process. Such weak acids are called **antioxidants**. Antioxidants are used as preservatives in many foods, paints, and fuels.

Fun Fact
You can speed up the browning process dramatically by placing the fruit in a blender and adding about 4 tablespoons of hydrogen peroxide. Blending exposes more of the aldehydes to the air and the peroxide releases oxygen. Once you have watched the show, carefully dispose of the mess. It is not safe to eat! It could make you very sick!

Merry Maggot Menagerie

Who couldn't use a few more friends? Here's a way to raise your own ghastly brood, then watch as they change right before your very eyes. This experiment should be started on a nice spring or summer day when fruit flies are plentiful.

Materials

- overripe fruit, such as a banana or apple
- clean quart jar
- cheesecloth (or one foot cut from a pair of panty hose—no holes in the toes!)
- rubber band
- magnifying glass

Directions

❶ Place the soon-to-be-rotten fruit in the open jar and put it in a safe, shady spot outside where it can sit undisturbed for at least 4 or 5 days.

❷ The day after you start your experiment, check the jar. If you see tiny black fruit flies bouncing around on the fruit, cover the top with a piece of cheesecloth or panty hose and secure with a rubber band. If no fruit flies are spotted, continue checking the jar each day until they appear.

❸ Once you've covered the jar, give the flies 2 days to enjoy their reeking meal and lay eggs. Then release them from the jar.

❹ Re-cover the jar with the cheesecloth or panty hose and store it in a warm place where no people or animals will touch it.

❺ Over the next 2 weeks, check the fruit in the jar every day with a magnifying glass without removing the cloth covering. With luck, you'll see a colony of fruit flies form and observe their progression from eggs (tiny, grayish specks) to adults.

How did this work?

Leaving ripening fruit out is like sounding a dinner bell for adult fruit flies. Not only do they gorge themselves on the sweet pulp, but they lay eggs there, too, to give their young a meal the moment they hatch. Like many other insects, fruit flies go through four stages of development.

The Four Stages of Development

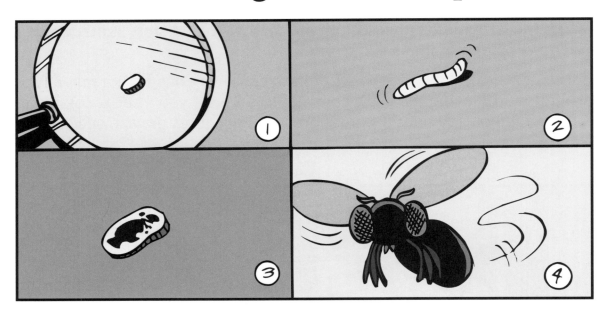

1. egg, 2. larva, 3. pupa, 4. adult

Fun Fact

The egg is the first stage. The second stage is the larva, which looks something like a small worm. In the fly, the larva is generally called a maggot. The third, or pupa stage, is a resting stage during which the insect develops its adult features. Finally, during the fourth stage, an adult fly emerges. The entire process is called **metamorphosis**. *Different kinds of insects go through the four stages of metamorphosis at different rates. For example, certain types lay eggs that hatch in hours, while others take days.*

Attack of the Night Crawlers

Believe it or not, you can help the environment by raising a crop of squirmy houseguests that are first-class recyclers. They eat nothing but garbage and leave behind something very useful for the garden: compost. Made up of decayed plant matter, compost is one of the best fertilizers you can find.

Materials

- hammer and nail
- plastic bin with tight-fitting lid (approximately 1 foot x 2 feet x 6 inches)
- base material (grass clippings, finely shredded newspaper, dried leaves)
- water
- 1 cup sand or soil
- approximately 24 earthworms
- scraps of fruit, vegetables, coffee grounds, eggshells, tea bags (Do not use meat or dairy products, or anything with sugar or salt in it.)

Directions

❶ With an adult's help, use the hammer and nail to poke 2 rows of holes in the sides of the container (at least 10 per side). Poke 10 or 12 holes in the bottom, too.

❷ Gather enough base material to fill the container a little more than half full. Dampen the material slightly with water, then, with your hands, mix in a cup of sand or soil. Be sure the material is situated loosely in the container, not packed.

❸ Place about two dozen earthworms, or night crawlers, into the container. (You can dig them up outside, or buy them at a store that sells live bait.) Set the container on blocks or bricks so that air can circulate around it. If you store it outside, find an area that is protected from wind, rain, and direct sunlight. It should also be in an area that won't be disturbed.

❹ Add approximately 2 cups of food scraps by lifting chunks of the base material and slipping scraps within. Put on the lid. As the worms use up the food, you'll need to add more. Each time you do, put the food in a different area of the bin. Gently blend the

scraps into the base material with your hands, being careful not to harm the tenants. Always wash your hands thoroughly after mixing. Repeat this step for 2 months. At that point you should find that much of the material in the bin has been converted into a dark, spongy "soil."

⑤ After 2 or 3 months your compost will be ready to use in a garden or in potted plants. Carefully remove the worms and release them in a safe place such as a garden or park, or put them aside while you set up a new batch of material for compost.

How did this work?

The earthworm is one of the original recyclers. It eats its own weight in decaying plant matter each day and passes out digested material, creating the world's best natural fertilizer. Another plus: Earthworms aerate the soil and create better drainage.

During the course of this experiment, if you feed your wiggly crew regularly and keep them in a place with good air circulation, the compost won't have anything but a rich, earthy smell. If it's stinky, you are probably giving the worms more scraps than they can handle. By the way, earthworms break down food scraps seven times faster than the material would break down without worms.

Fun Fact
Some people are squeamish about handling earthworms. That's easy to understand if you live in Australia. One earthworm species there can grow to 11 feet in length!

Putrid, Pungent Punch

If you can stand the stench, this foul-smelling fluid is a useful acid-testing indicator.

Materials

- knife
- half of a red cabbage
- pot
- 1 quart distilled water
- colander or sieve
- measuring cup
- 3 small glass jars with lids
- label
- marker
- measuring spoons
- 1 tablespoon lemon juice
- $\frac{1}{4}$ teaspoon baking soda

Directions

❶ With an adult's help, cut the cabbage into small, bite-sized pieces and place in a pot. Pour in the distilled water and bring to a full boil. Turn off the heat and allow the fluid to cool. (The smell of this experiment will become apparent here!)

❷ Pour the cooled liquid through a colander into a measuring cup. (You can use the cabbage in your compost heap [see page 39], or eat it with a little butter and salt. It is a good source of vitamins A and C, as well as calcium. Besides, it tastes great.)

❸ The cabbage water will be an inky blue. Pour it into the first glass jar and label it *cabbage indicator*.

❹ Pour about $\frac{1}{4}$ cup of cabbage indicator into another glass jar, then add the tablespoon of lemon juice. The indicator will turn bright pink in the presence of acid.

❺ Pour about $\frac{1}{4}$ cup of cabbage indicator into the last glass jar. Add $\frac{1}{4}$ teaspoon of baking soda. The indicator turns dark green in the presence of a base (a substance that reacts with acid to form a salt).

❻ Using the same process, test other foods to see if you can detect an acid or a base. Coffee, vinegar, and milk are good foods to test.

How did this work?

The hot water releases chemicals from the cabbage, some of which appear blue. When the chemicals come in contact with an acid or a **base**, a chemical reaction changes the color of the fluid from blue to pink or green. By carefully watching for any changes in the color of the indicator, you can detect even small amounts of acid or base in the substance you are testing.

Bloated Raisin Bugs

In just a matter of hours, you can turn a handful of innocent raisins into a herd of what look like bloated water bugs. Then you can really freak out your friends by eating one!

Materials

- pint- or quart-sized glass jar
- warm water
- 12 to 15 raisins, any kind

Directions

❶ Fill the glass jar within 2 inches of the top rim with lukewarm tap water.

❷ Drop the raisins into the jar, then place the jar where it can be left undisturbed. Let the experiment sit overnight or for at least 6 hours.

3 When the time is up, check your results. Instead of being tiny and shriveled, the raisins are now fat and bloated. Reach in and squeeze a couple. How did they get so heavy and squishy?

How did this work?

You are observing an example of **osmosis**. Water naturally moves from areas of greater concentration to areas of lesser **concentration**. In this case, the water travels through a **membrane**, the raisin skin. When you first put the raisins in the jar, lots of water was outside of each dried-up raisin and not much inside. The water moved through tiny openings in the raisin skin deep into the raisin itself, making it heavy, soft, and bloated.

Fun Fact

If you sit in a tub of water for a long time, your fingers probably will get wrinkly. Why doesn't your whole body undergo the same change? While you're in the tub, your skin will absorb some water, but much of your skin is partly protected from absorbing water by an oily substance called sebum. This substance is produced by tiny glands known as sebaceous glands. They occur all over the body, except in the skin of your fingertips and toes. As a result, water enters those areas by osmosis, and the skin there becomes wrinkly like a prune and puffy.

Try to figure out a way to prevent osmosis from taking place in this experiment. Hint: As sebum helps keep water from being absorbed through our skin, think of a substance that could do the same for the raisins. How about dipping the raisins in oil or painting them with clear nail polish before you begin? Try it and see!

A Hairy Sponge

This unusual garden grows so fast it will stand your hair on end. But can it really survive without soil?

Materials

- seeds (such as radish or alfalfa)
- small bowl
- water
- strainer
- kitchen sponge
- saucer
- spray bottle of water

Directions

❶ Place a handful of seeds in a small bowl and cover them with water. Let the seeds soak for about an hour, then pour them into a strainer to separate them from the water.

❷ Soak the sponge for a few moments in water, wring it out, and place it in the saucer.

❸ Sprinkle a handful of the wet seeds from the strainer on the sponge and poke them down into the openings.

❹ Place the saucer in a warm area, but not in direct sunlight. Using the spray bottle, keep the sponge moist over the next 2 or 3 days. The seeds will soon sprout, and tiny hairlike plants will shoot up. When your garden needs a trim, just munch away. It should stay fresh for a week or two.

How did this work?

Most plants make their own food with sunlight, air, and water in a process called **photosynthesis**. As they grow, they get other nutrients they need from the soil. When seed-bearing plants first begin to sprout, they are unable to use photosynthesis to produce food because their leaves are too immature to do so. Seeds, however, have a limited food supply inside them that helps get the new plants started. Once this food supply is used up, the seeds fall away from the new plants and decay. In this experiment the tiny plants in the sponge use the stored food in the seeds to get started. If you want to keep the plants going longer than a week or so, add a few drops of liquid fertilizer to the sponge or transplant them to your garden.

Fun Fact

Seeds come in all sizes. The world's smallest seeds are those of certain orchids. They are so tiny that it takes more than 28 million of them to weigh an ounce. The heaviest seed is that of the coco-de-mer, found on the Seychelles Islands in the Indian Ocean. A single seed of this plant may weigh 44 pounds. Imagine trying to plant a row of those in your garden!

Bucket of Bacteria

The world would be a much stinkier place if we didn't bathe or brush our teeth. Here's a way to see why.

Materials

- ½ cup water
- saucepan
- small heat-proof bowl
- 4 packets unflavored gelatin
- mixing spoon
- glass jar with lid
- cotton swab

Directions

❶ Bring the water to a boil in saucepan, then, after it cools for a few minutes, pour carefully into the bowl.

❷ Sprinkle the 4 packets of gelatin into the bowl and stir until the powder dissolves.

❸ Pour the mixture into the jar, screw the lid on tightly, and set the jar on its side in a safe spot where it won't roll. Wait about 4 or 5 hours for the gelatin to set. (It is not necessary to put it in the refrigerator.)

❹ Now you need to find some bacteria. You won't have to look far! Take off your shoes and socks and rub the cotton swab between your toes. Now brush the swab across the gelatin in four long, separate strokes, then close the jar again and leave it in a warm, dark place for a few days.

❺ When you check your experiment, you won't see the bacteria, but you will see lines in the gelatin. The gelatin is what the bacteria have been eating. Now open the jar and stand back. The contents of the jar will smell terrible!

❻ When you are finished, dump the gelatin down the drain, followed by a rinse of hot water. Wash your hands and the inside of the jar thoroughly with soap and water.

❼ Repeat the steps again, but use a different source of bacteria. How about from your mouth or hands? Do you think you could collect bacteria from just-washed hands?

How did this work?

There are billions of tiny organisms living on and around us called *bacteria*. Some are helpful, others are harmful, and still others are somewhere in between. For example, some bacteria on humans are responsible for unpleasant odors in the mouth, underarms, and feet.

The gelatin you prepared makes a good food source for such bacteria. It is called a *growth medium*. It allows the bacteria to reproduce easily, and you get the concentrated effect when you open the jar to smell it.

Fun Fact

Bacteria are microscopic, single-celled **organisms**. *Some are so tiny that it would take 50,000 of them to cover a square inch. They can also reproduce rapidly. Under ideal conditions, a single bacterium could possibly produce 3 billion new cells in a single day!*

Some very deadly diseases are caused by bacteria, including tetanus, leprosy, scarlet fever, and tuberculosis. On the other hand, life as we know it could not exist without certain bacteria, such as those that live in the human digestive system and help break down our food.

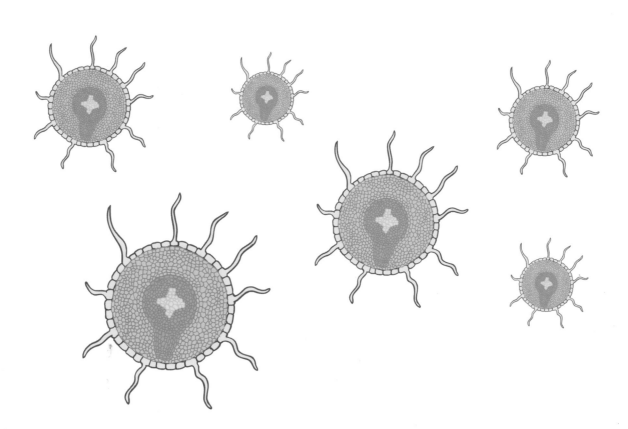

A Fungus Among Us

Here's an idea for a particularly disgusting gag lunch—a mold sandwich. No joke . . . the musty odor can really make you gag!

Materials

- slice of bread
- 1 teaspoon water
- small, flat plate
- self-sealing sandwich bag
- label
- pen
- notepad

Directions

❶ To dampen the slice of bread, pour the teaspoon of water on a flat plate and spread it around, getting as much of the plate wet as possible. Then lay the bread in it. If needed, sprinkle a little more water on the bread with a spoon.

❷ Remove the moist bread from the plate, slip it into the sandwich bag, and fasten the bag shut.

3 Put the bag in a warm, dark place for one week—a closet or cupboard will work. Label the bag with a warning such as *experiment in progress* to let your family know that it is an experiment and not lunch. Whatever you do, don't forget about it!

4 Check once a day, every day, to see how the fungus is developing. If you wish, you can draw sketches or make notes about what you see so you have a record of the progress of the experiment. This will make it easier to see how quickly the fungus grows from day to day. At the end of the week you should find that the bread is covered with a layer of mold.

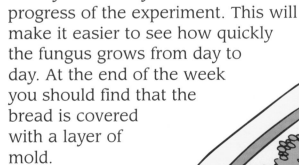

How did this work?

Mold is a kind of **fungus**. It grows from spores (tiny cells with hard coverings) that are so small that they float on air. Even though you can't see them, spores are already on the bread before you put it in the bag. By putting water on the bread and placing it in a cupboard, you are creating the warm, damp environment that helps spores grow. Unlike green plants, fungi do not make their own food from sunlight, air, and water. Fungi live by absorbing food from other sources. *Fungus* is from a Latin term meaning "food-robbing."

Fun Fact

*Penicillin is an important life-saving medicine known as an **antibiotic**. Penicillin is produced by a mold. In 1928 a British scientist named Alexander Fleming noticed that a certain mold stopped the growth of bacteria. It took many years, but scientists finally isolated the important element that fought infection. Since then, penicillin—first discovered in a lowly mold—has helped save millions of lives.*

Jeepers, Check Those Creeping Peepers

The small spud sits quietly in a corner. But what's happening? Are those long, spindly tentacles sprouting out of its eyes? It's the attack of the killer potato!

Materials

- potato, any kind with eyes
- knife
- clean jar or glass with opening wide enough to fit potato
- 4 toothpicks
- water

Directions

❶ Check your potato for firmness. It should be hard with no dark, soft, rotten spots. With an adult's help, slice off the lower third of the potato. (You can dispose of it or save it for a smaller version of this experiment.) Stick four toothpicks securely in the larger piece, spacing them evenly around the potato about $\frac{1}{2}$ inch above the bottom flat end.

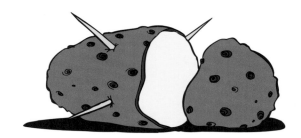

❷ Fill the jar nearly to the rim with cool tap water. Place the cut end of the potato in the water, with the toothpicks resting on the jar's opening.

❸ Put the jar in a warm place that gets sunlight for at least an hour or two each day. Check every other day to be sure the water continues to cover the cut end of the potato.

❹ In about a week the potato will sprout leaves and roots from little depressions known as *eyes*. If you want to keep your new plant, let it grow to about 6 inches tall, then plant about an inch of the root end of the potato in a pot of soil. Place it in a sunny location, keeping the soil moist, and your pet plant will flourish.

How did this work?

Vegetative propagation, demonstrated in this experiment, is the term for growing a new plant from a part of an adult plant rather than from seeds or **spores**.

Although a potato grows underground, it is not a root or a seed. It is actually a tuber, or food storage unit, for the potato plant. A tuber is the enlarged end of an underground stem. When conditions are right, the eyes on the potato can sprout leaves and roots, growing into a new plant. At first, the plant is nourished by the "meat" of the potato (the part we eat), which is mostly water, starch, and some **protein**. Once the new young plant is well established with a system of leaves and roots, it is nourished by the soil that it is planted in.

Fun Fact

If you wanted to grow potatoes in your garden, you probably would not plant seeds, because potato plants grown from seeds can vary tremendously. Instead you would plant small pieces of potato called sets. Each set must include at least one eye. The plants grown from pieces of potato are identical to the parent plant. It's almost like cloning in your own backyard!

Muggy, Muddy Waters

Create a murky swamp, then clean it up without even breaking a sweat. (Just wait until you see the muddy mess this experiment leaves behind!)

Materials

- 2 cereal bowls
- water
- 2 tablespoons of dirt
- mixing spoon
- brick (or shoe box)
- white handkerchief

Directions

❶ Fill one cereal bowl halfway with water, then add 2 tablespoons of dirt and stir well.

❷ Put the brick (or upside-down shoe box) on a flat surface and set the bowl of muddy water on top of it. Place the empty second bowl on the flat surface next to the brick, so it rests several inches below the muddy water.

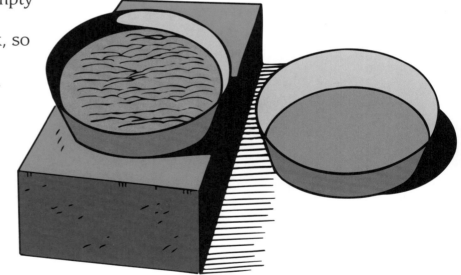

❸ Roll the handkerchief into a tube, tight enough to stay rolled up. Place one end of the handkerchief in the muddy water and the other end in the empty bowl, not quite touching the bottom.

4 Wait 24 hours, then check the experiment. How did the water get into the once-empty bowl? Where is the dirt?

How did this work?

You are looking at an example of **capillary action**. Say what? It's like this: The cloth is made up of tiny fibers with air spaces in between. The water slowly creeps up into the spaces, a little higher on the sides than in the middle, giving the water level a cup shape. The water molecules attract each other, soon drawing the center of the water surface up the cloth, causing the entire waterline to become level. When that happens, the water on the sides creeps up again and so on, until the water makes it over the edge of the bowl. Gravity takes over and the water slowly seeps down the hanky, finally dripping into the lower bowl. The dirt is left behind because it's too heavy to hitch a ride up the hanky.

Important! No matter how clean the water in the lower bowl looks, don't drink it. The dirt may have been too heavy to make the trip, but lightweight **bacteria** might have hitched a ride and could make you sick if you drink the water.

Fun Fact

Water rises in plant stems and tree trunks by capillary action. For some trees, the journey of the water to the top is a pretty impressive trip. For example, the tallest tree in the United States stands in Redwood National Park, Orick, California, and measures more than 365 feet tall.

Wiggle and Squirm

Amaze your friends by using capillary action to turn a plain paper wrapper into a wiggly worm.

Materials

- drinking straw with a paper wrapper
- cup of water

Directions

❶ Hold the wrapped straw upright on a tabletop. Tear the paper wrapper from the exposed tip.

❷ Slide the wrapper down so that it bunches up around the base of the straw. Slip the wrapper off and place the tightly squeezed paper on its side on the tabletop.

❸ Dip one end of the straw about $\frac{1}{2}$-inch deep into the cup of water. Capture a few drops of water in the straw by placing your index finger over the open end.

❹ Hold the straw over the scrunched wrapper and carefully drip water along its length. What happened?

How did this work?

The paper seems to wriggle and squirm as if it were alive! The process at work here is capillary action. Paper and cloth are made up of tiny fibers that have small spaces in between them. These fibers absorb, or suck up, the water by a process called capillary action. Water molecules move through the spaces adhering to the fibers. As the water molecules move along the fibers, they attract other water molecules. As the crunched fibers in the paper wrapper soak up water, they straighten out and the paper lengthens.

Moaning Marvin

When Marvin gets going, the whine of his wooden head can send chills up and down your spine.

Materials

- rectangle of pine or other light wood, approximately 8 inches long, 2 inches wide, and $\frac{1}{4}$ inch thick
- 3-foot length of $\frac{1}{8}$-inch-thick string
- drill or hammer and large nail
- colored markers

Directions

❶ Ask an adult to help you make a hole in one end of the block of wood just large enough to pass the string through. Using a drill is the easiest way, but it also can be done with a hammer and a large nail.

❷ Draw a scary face on the wood with the markers.

❸ Pass the string through the hole and tie the end securely with double knots. Have an adult check your work—you don't want to launch Marvin into orbit in the middle of the experiment!

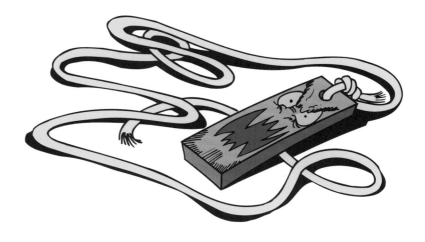

❹ To perform the experiment you must move outside, at least 10 feet away from buildings, trees, and people. Grip the loose end of the string and whirl the wood in a large circle above your head. Check out the spooky moaning sound Marvin makes!

How did this work?

There are a couple of things at work here. The moaning **sound** is created because the wood and cord vibrate as they move through the air, causing the surrounding air to vibrate. These air vibrations travel in waves and eventually strike a membrane in your ear called your *eardrum*. The vibrations are then passed on to nerve endings in your inner ear and you hear the vibrations as sound. Because Marvin is moving in a circle, the vibrations repeat at intervals that make a sound like a moan.

The force that keeps Marvin going in a circle instead of flying off into space is called **centripetal force**. Objects tend to want to keep moving in a straight line, unless a force makes them change direction. Your arm and the string are applying that force to Marvin.

Fun Fact

*If you slow down or speed up, you can change the **pitch** of the moan. Pitch is a measure of the **frequency** of vibrations. Try spinning Marvin at different speeds to see how the sound changes.*

Sneaky Snakes

What could be scarier than hearing the rattle of a rattlesnake? Holding the source of that disturbing sound in your hands!

Materials

- needle-nose pliers
- piece of strong wire about 5 inches long (coat-hanger wire works well)
- two 3-inch-long rubber bands
- metal washer, approximately 1 inch in diameter
- paper coin-envelope
- pencil
- an unsuspecting friend

Directions

❶ Using the pliers, curl the two ends of the wire as shown. Make a small bend in the center of the wire, forming an open-ended triangle.

❷ Thread one rubber band halfway through the hole in the washer, then hook both ends of the band onto one curved end of the wire. Repeat the process on the other wire end with the second rubber band, threading it through the same washer.

❸ Take the coin envelope and write BEWARE: Snake! in large letters. Now turn the washer about twenty times as you would turn the winder on a windup toy. Slip the entire contraption into the coin envelope, being careful not to let the bands unwind. Keep the washer flat and slip the flap of the envelope inside.

❹ Hand your prepared envelope to a friend and say, "Open this envelope if you dare!" Your friend will have to reach in to pull out the flap. That will release the washer and it will spin, making a disturbing rattlesnake sound in the paper envelope.

How did this work?

This experiment is a demonstration of potential and kinetic **energy**. Energy is the ability to do work. **Potential energy** is the possible energy something has because of its position. When the position changes, the object can accomplish work. For example, a ball at the top of a staircase has potential energy. Give it a nudge, and as the ball tumbles down the stairs, its potential energy changes to **kinetic energy**. Kinetic energy is the energy of motion, or energy that is at work. In Sneaky Snakes, the washer and the tightly wound rubber bands have potential energy until the washer is released, then the spinning washer and unwinding rubber bands have kinetic energy.

Fun Fact

Energy can be stored in two main ways. One is the potential energy a body has because of its position. Another way energy can be stored is as **chemical energy**, *or the energy stored in an* **atom** *or molecule, which can be released through a* **chemical reaction**. *Examples of stored chemical energy are gas in a car or food in your body. When you run around, the chemical energy in the food you have eaten is released. About 25 percent of it is changed to kinetic energy. Most of it is converted to heat so the body has to find ways to cool itself down. Which brings us to a gross side-effect of using up all this energy—sweat. In fact, if you lived in a hot climate and played hard all day, you could sweat out as much as 12 quarts of fluid in a day.*

Experiment Log

Record each experiment that you perform. Rate the gross and annoying results for each experiment using the following scale:

1 = Not so	**2** = Sort of	**3** = Just	**4** = Really	**5** = Super

	Date	Experiment	Gross Rating	Annoyance Rating
1.				
2.				
3.				
4.				
5.				
6.				
7.				
8.				
9.				
10.				
11.				
12.				
13.				
14.				
15.				
16.				
17.				
18.				
19.				
20.				
21.				
22.				
23.				
24.				
25.				
26.				
27.				

Read, Sing, and Play Along! Gross and Annoying Songs

Gross Recipes

Before You Bake

The following recipes contain all the ideas and kitchen help every budding gross gourmand needs to know. You'll find loads of recipes that are fun to make and even more fun to serve.

Get off to a good start by learning on the following pages important cooking terms as well as safety tips. When you see a recipe you'd like to make, read through it before you begin. Then gather all the ingredients and tools.

For some kitchen tools, such as measuring cups, take care to use the proper type. Liquids pour easily and accurately with a liquid-measuring cup. Be sure to check the measurements at eye level. Dry ingredient should be measured using stackable dry-measuring cups. Level them off using a spatula or butter knife for exact measuring. Because almost every recipe calls for measuring tools of some kind, measuring cups and measuring spoons have not been included under "Tools You'll Need." Always keep a selection handy.

Also, when required, be sure to prepare any tools properly, such as greasing your baking sheet. Place a small amount of butter or shortening on the baking sheet and thinly spread it over the surface using a clean paper towel, or simply coat the surface with nonstick cooking spray. In either case, if the recipe calls for a greased pan, it is important to coat the pan's entire surface so that food doesn't stick when baking.

Many recipes suggest microwave cooking instructions. Microwaves can vary in their cooking times, depending on their size and power. This book suggests cooking times based on the most commonly used power levels, 600 to 650 watts. If you're trying a recipe for the first time, be sure to check for doneness at regular intervals while heating any food item. If you do not have access to a microwave, alternate cooking suggestions are given. However, they will require different cooking tools, so be sure to go over the recipe with an adult first.

All the recipes have been kitchen-tested and tasted and are wholly suitable for anyone who loves to eat good food—even if it does happen to look gross! Dig in!

A Baker's Dozen Rules

1. Always work with an adult, especially when using the oven or stove, or any electrical appliance.

2. Read through your recipe thoroughly to make sure you have all the necessary ingredients and tools and enough time to prepare it.

3. Dress the part! Tie back long hair, fold up shirt sleeves, and wear an apron or old shirt over your clothes.

4. An adult should always be supervising when you are using knives or scissors.

5. Keep a fire extinguisher in your kitchen and know how to use it.

6. Wash your hands thoroughly before cooking and frequently as you handle various foods and utensils.

7. Turn saucepan handles to the side so they won't get knocked off the stove. Lift saucepan lids away from your face to avoid steam burns.

8. Have an adult check over your kitchen tools. Dull knives cause far more accidents than sharp ones, so be sure yours are in good condition!

9. Never leave the kitchen when something is cooking on the stovetop.

10. Keep food safe from bacteria. Start with clean counters and tools. Keep refrigerated foods chilled until you're ready to use them. Never place cooked foods or foods that will be eaten raw on surfaces or in containers that held raw meats or eggs. Always refrigerate uneaten foods as soon as possible.

11. Always use thick, dry pot holders to handle hot pans, pots, baking sheets, or baking dishes.

12. Check all ingredients for freshness before using by sniffing them and examining them for mold or spoilage. Ask an adult to help you.

13. When you're finished preparing your creations, clean the kitchen and wash all the tools you used. This way you're sure to be welcomed back into the kitchen for a repeat performance!

Words to Know

baking sheet – a flat pan with no sides on it, designed for even heating of items, such as cookies

boil – to heat liquid to the point where air bubbles form at the bottom of the pan

candy "eyes" – made from hard sugar, these candies are available in many sizes at cake-decorating supply stores and many craft supply stores

colander – a bowl with tiny holes used for washing and draining food

confectionery coating (also called candy-making chocolate) – a chocolate designed to stay smooth and evenly textured when melted

cutting board – a plastic mat or wooden block designed to protect countertops from damage while chopping or cutting

dash – a very slight addition of an ingredient, such as one sprinkle

divided – when an ingredient is separated into smaller amounts and added at different times

double boiler – a double saucepan designed to be filled with water in the lower portion and cooking ingredients in the upper portion. The heated water warms food slowly, preventing it from burning.

upper portion
for ingredients

lower portion
contains water

dry-measuring cups – often made of plastic and designed so that ingredients can be scooped, then leveled off with a rubber spatula or butter knife. Dry-measuring cups come in stacked sizes ranging from $\frac{1}{8}$ cup to 2 cups.

electric mixer – an electrical appliance, often handheld, that's designed to mix ingredients quickly. Note: If you don't have one, most recipes can be mixed by hand with a wooden spoon, whisk, or heavy-duty rubber spatula.

fold – to combine light ingredients gently, such as whipped cream, with heavier ingredients, such as fruit, with minimal mixing

handheld bottle opener – a small tool about 4 inches long, with a pointed end for poking holes in cans and a rounded end for popping tops from bottles

heat-safe work surface – a work surface that is either protected from heat with a pot holder or is naturally resistant to heat

invert – to flip over and empty a pan or tray onto another surface, such as a cake plate or cutting board

jimmie cake-decorating sprinkles – tiny, hot-dog-shaped decorating candies, most often sprinkled over baked goods (available in single colors, mixed colors, or chocolate)

knead – to smooth and mix dough by folding it over and over using your hands and knuckles

line – to cover the interior of a baking sheet, pan, or bowl with removable protection, such as waxed paper or plastic wrap

liquid-measuring cups – usually made of clear plastic or glass and designed with a spout for pouring liquid measurements

microwave-safe container – container made of glass, plastic, or paper, safe for use in the microwave. (Never use metal, metal-trimmed, Styrofoam®, or hand-blown glass containing air bubbles)

mix – to blend ingredients evenly by either stirring or beating

mixing bowl – a bowl that is deep enough for electric beaters to fit in without splattering ingredients over the sides. (Mixing bowls come in a variety of sizes.)

nonpareils – tiny candy balls available in many colors for sprinkling on baked goods

paring knife – a small, sharp knife with a short narrow blade used for slicing and carving

peel – the outer skin of the fruit or vegetables, or the action of removing the outer skin from fruit or vegetables

rubber spatula - a flat rubber tool with a long handle and flexible tip, used for scraping bowls and evenly spreading ingredients, such as frosting

serrated knife – a knife with jagged teeth much like those on a saw, best used for cutting dry items like bread

set – when ingredients, such as gelatin, are firm and solid throughout

sieve – a bowl-shaped utensil with a handle and fine-mesh interior used for separating solid foods from liquid or semi liquid ingredients

tongs – a tool used for picking up or turning hot items while cooling or dipping

utility knife – a 6- to 8-inch knife with a smooth, sharp blade

whisk – to whip or mix ingredients using a wire tool (also called a whisk)

wooden spoon – a spoon made of wood used for stirring and mixing

Equivalency Charts

Abbreviations

tsp = teaspoon	T = tablespoon	c = Cup	fl oz = fluid ounce
pt = pint	qt = quart	gal = gallon	

U.S. Customary Measures and Weights

Dash	less than $\frac{1}{8}$ tsp	16 T	1 c or 8 fl oz
3 tsp	1 T	1 c	8 fl oz
2 T	$\frac{1}{8}$ c or 1 fl oz	2 c	1 pt or 16 fl oz
4 T	$\frac{1}{4}$ c or 2 fl oz	4 c	1 qt
$5\frac{1}{3}$ T	$\frac{1}{3}$ c or 2.67 fl oz	2 pt	1 qt or 32 fl oz
8 T	$\frac{1}{2}$ c or 4 fl oz	4 qt	1 gal
12 T	$\frac{3}{4}$ c or 6 fl oz		

U.S. Customary to Metric

Fluid Ounces	U.S.	Milliliters
-	1 tsp	5
$\frac{1}{4}$	2 tsp	10
$\frac{1}{2}$	1 T	14
1	2 T	28
2	$\frac{1}{4}$ c	56
4	$\frac{1}{2}$ c	110
6	$\frac{3}{4}$ c	170
8	1 c	225
9	-	250, $\frac{1}{4}$ liter
16	2 c	450
18	$2\frac{1}{4}$ c	500, $\frac{1}{2}$ liter
24	3 c	675
32	4 c or 1 qt	900
36	$4\frac{1}{2}$ c	1000, 1 liter

Oven Temperatures

Fahrenheit	Celsius
225	110
250	130
275	140
300	150
325	170
350	180
375	190
400	200
425	220
450	230
475	240
500	250

Read, Sing, and Play Along! Gross and Annoying Songs

Nasty Nibbles

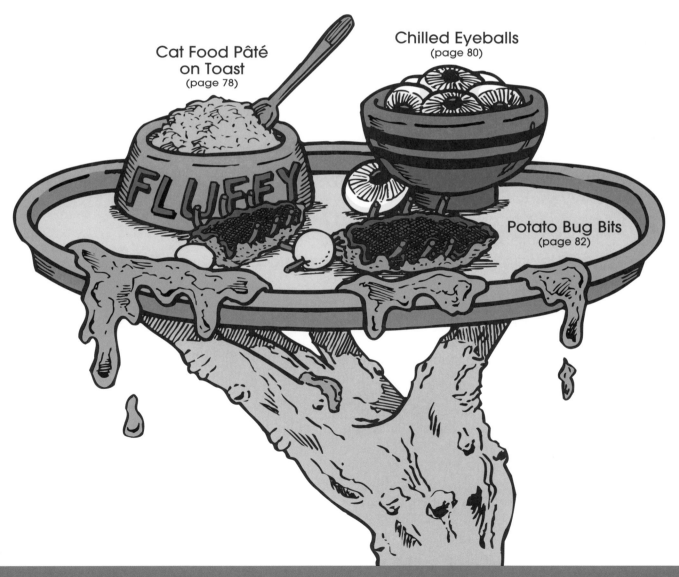

Cat Food Pâté
on Toast
(page 78)

Chilled Eyeballs
(page 80)

Potato Bug Bits
(page 82)

FLUFFY

Read, Sing, and Play Along! Gross and Annoying Songs

Eye Boogers

Eyes sealed tight with crusty boogers? Don't despair! Rub your peepers over a platter and harvest those crunchy pale green treats to serve to your friends.

INGREDIENTS

$\frac{1}{2}$ cup sugar
$\frac{1}{4}$ cup water
$\frac{1}{4}$ teaspoon almond extract
Yellow and green food coloring
3 cups mini marshmallows

TOOLS YOU'LL NEED

- small mixing bowl
- fork
- waxed paper
- clean spray bottle

1. Place the sugar into the small mixing bowl and blend together with a fork. Lay two sheets of waxed paper (each about 12 inches long) side by side on your work surface.

2. Pour water and almond extract into spray bottle. (Use a new spray bottle for cooking- *never use one that's been used for cleaning products.*) Add two drops of yellow food coloring and one drop of green. Attach spray top to bottle and gently shake to blend the colors.

3. Spread about $\frac{1}{2}$ cup mini marshmallows onto one sheet of the waxed paper. Lightly but completely mist them with your water-filled spray bottle. Turn them over and mist the bottoms.

4. Pick up a small handful of moistened mini marshmallows and drop them into the sugar to create larger-than-life crusty eye boogers. Roll them with your fingers to coat evenly, then place them on the second sheet of waxed paper to dry. Repeat with remaining ingredients.

5. After about one hour, turn them over so that the eye boogers can dry evenly on all sides. These get more chewy with age, so if you're planning a party, you can make them a day or two ahead of time and store them, lightly covered, at room temperature.

Serves: 8 sleepy eaters ($\frac{1}{4}$ rounded cup for each)

Freaky Fact

Real eye boogers begin life as lubricating moisture for your eyes, more commonly referred to as tears. Not only are they made of water, but they also contain albumin, ammonia, citric acid, salts, sugar, urea, and more!

Sputum Chewies

What do you do with that wonderfully slimy, sticky blob you've coughed up? Don't waste it! Gather that flying phlegm and save it for your next party.

INGREDIENTS

3 envelopes unflavored gelatin
$1\frac{1}{4}$ cups water, divided
$1\frac{1}{2}$ cups sugar
$\frac{1}{4}$ teaspoon peppermint extract

Stove Top
TOOLS YOU'LL NEED

- small mixing bowl
- mixing spoon
- medium saucepan with lid
- whisk
- pot holder
- baking sheet
- waxed paper

1. In a small mixing bowl, stir the gelatin into $\frac{1}{2}$ cup water. Let mixture stand for five minutes to dissolve.

2. With an adult's help, bring the sugar and remaining $\frac{3}{4}$ cup water to a boil in a medium saucepan. Stir constantly with the whisk to prevent burning.

3. Add the dissolved gelatin mixture to the saucepan and reduce heat. Simmer, stirring constantly, for five minutes.

4. With a pot holder, have an adult help you remove the saucepan from the heat and place it on a heat-safe work surface. Add the peppermint extract to give the sputum a slightly minty flavor. Blend thoroughly and allow ingredients to cool slightly. Then cover the pan and place it in the refrigerator for about 30 minutes to chill.

5. When the gelatin has partially thickened, use the whisk to lightly whip in natural looking air bubbles into your sputum mixture. Line a baking sheet with waxed paper. Scoop generous tablespoonfuls of the gelatin onto the waxed paper. Leave about 2 inches between each sputum wad to allow for spreading. Set baking sheet in refrigerator for two hours or until firm.

6. Remove from refrigerator and let sputum stand at room temperature for three to four hours, turning over every hour with your clean hands, so both sides dry evenly. You can eat them now or cover unused sputum chewies tightly with plastic wrap and store them in the refrigerator. These are a great do-ahead party treat. You can make these up to one week in advance.

Makes: About 1 pound of hacked-up sputum (enough for 10 to 12 people)

Roach on a Coach

Don't freak out if there's a giant cockroach crawling on your food—he is the food!

INGREDIENTS

4 large carrots
8 oil-cured black olives with pits
canned American cheese

TOOLS YOU'LL NEED

- nontoxic black felt-tip marker
- 32 toothpicks
- vegetable peeler
- utility knife
- paring knife

1. With a black felt-tip marker, color 16 toothpicks black and set them aside for use later as your roach antennae.

2. With an adult's help, use a vegetable peeler to peel the carrots. Cut the ends off of each and discard. Starting at the widest portion of each carrot, use the utility knife to cut eight thin coin shapes, each about $\frac{3}{4}$-inch thick. These will be the car's wheels. Next, cut the remaining part of each carrot in half lengthwise. You will have eight carrot sticks, about 3 to 4 inches each, to be used as the car bodies, and 32 round coin shapes to be used as wheels for your eight cars.

3. To create a car axle with wheels, poke one carrot round onto each end of an uncolored toothpick. Repeat with the remaining uncolored toothpicks and carrot rounds. Set them aside.

4. To create crawling roaches, have an adult help you use a paring knife to cut an olive lengthwise about two-thirds down the center. Leave the remaining portion attached as the roach's head. Gently fan the olive meat away from the pit to form the roach's wings and body. Do not remove the pit. Repeat with the remaining olives.

5. Place one carrot-stick car body onto your work surface. Place the roach onto the middle of the car. To secure the roach in place, carefully but firmly poke two black-colored toothpicks through the head portion into the car so that about half of each toothpick extends out as an antenna.

6. To assemble, place two sets of wheels onto your work surface. Lay a roach-covered car on top of each pair of axles, then carefully slide the carrot wheels toward the carrot car body, so they hug up against the side of the car. To add larvae (baby roaches), place a generous squirt of American cheese underneath the roach, plus two more additional squirts behind it. They're ready to eat now. (This treat can be made a day in advance and kept tightly covered in the refrigerator.)

Serves: 8 roach relatives

Freaky Fact
Largest cockroach on record? It is 3.81 inches long—that's probably bigger than the palm of your hand! Forget the bug spray—you'd better start running if you cross paths with this one!

Cat Food Pâté on Toast

Who would have thought a can of ground-up intestines, fish eyes, and chicken heads and feet, covered with a coagulated, jiggling layer of slime, could taste so good? Here's a delicious variation on a feline favorite for those who "purrr-fur" copycat cat food to the real thing!

INGREDIENTS

6.75-ounce can deviled ham
8 slices processed American cheese
1 to 2 tablespoons Dijon mustard
1 envelope unflavored gelatin
crackers

Microwave/Stove Top
TOOLS YOU'LL NEED

- microwave-safe mixing bowl
- fork
- plastic wrap
- bowl
- empty margarine tub, 1-cup size
- cooking spray
- rubber spatula
- new, unused cat food bowl

1. Empty the can of deviled ham into a microwave-safe mixing bowl, and use a fork to lightly fluff the ham. Break up the American cheese into bite-size pieces and fold them into the ham. Add the mustard and blend.

2. Cover bowl loosely with plastic wrap. Place the bowl into the microwave. Heat on high (100%) for about 45 seconds or until the cheese has melted. Ask an adult to help you remove it from the microwave and set it aside to cool slightly. (This mixture may also be warmed in a small saucepan on low heat with an adult's help. Stir continuously until cheese is melted and all the ingredients are thoroughly blended.)

3. With an adult's help, dissolve the gelatin in a bowl as directed on the package. To congeal the gelatin slightly, place it in the refrigerator for about 10 minutes.

4. Lightly coat the inside of an empty margarine tub with cooking spray. Use your spatula to scoop the deviled ham mixture into the tub. This will be your cat food can mold. Press down lightly with your spatula to remove air pockets, then invert the tub into your cat food bowl. If the cat food does not come out, gently but firmly tap the bottom of the plastic tub.

5. Pour the slightly congealed gelatin mixture over the top of your Cat Food Pâté. Then place the bowl in the refrigerator to continue setting the gelatin (about 30 minutes). Serve immediately with crackers or cover tightly with plastic wrap. Can be stored up to five days in advance.

Serves: 8 fancy feasters

Putrid Presentation

Cats go wild for catnip! Use your kitchen scissors to snip chives into inch-long pieces for catnip as a glorious garnish to your Cat Food Pâté. Arrange it decoratively along the edge of your serving platter.

Chilled Eyeballs

A treat just perfect for sucking on!

INGREDIENTS

$\frac{2}{3}$ cup water
1 small box flavored gelatin
$\frac{1}{4}$ cup shredded coconut
2 envelopes unflavored (clear) gelatin
2 cups milk
1 large package vanilla-flavored instant pudding and pie filling mix
24 black mini jelly beans

Stove Top

TOOLS YOU'LL NEED

- paper towels
- vegetable oil
- 2 plastic egg-holding trays (from your refrigerator)
- small saucepan
- whisk
- medium mixing bowl
- plastic wrap
- warm, moist towel
- small rubber spatula
- serving platter

1. Moisten a section of paper towel with vegetable oil and rub it along the inside of each clean egg holder to prevent sticking. Be sure to coat each section thoroughly.

2. With an adult's help, bring $\frac{2}{3}$ cup water to a boil in a saucepan. Remove from heat and stir in the flavored gelatin using a whisk. Continue stirring for about two minutes or until completely dissolved. Spoon $1\frac{1}{2}$ to 2 teaspoons dissolved flavored gelatin into each egg holder. Top each with a pinch of coconut (about $\frac{1}{4}$ teaspoon). Place the egg trays into the refrigerator to chill for exactly 40 minutes.

3. After about 30 minutes, begin preparing the "whites" of the eyes. Pour the unflavored gelatin into a liquid-measuring cup and dissolve gelatin according to the instructions on the package.

4. Pour the milk and instant pudding mix into a medium mixing bowl along with the dissolved gelatin. Whisk vigorously to blend ingredients completely. Set aside.

5. When the flavored gelatin has set for exactly 40 minutes, remove trays from the refrigerator and fill each egg holder to the rim with the pudding mixture. Refrigerate any excess pudding for snacking on later. The trays will be full, so carefully place them back in the refrigerator to chill for two to three hours. If you're not planning on serving these immediately, cover trays with plastic wrap and store, refrigerated, for up to one week.

6. An hour or two before you serve the eyeballs, carefully remove them from the egg trays. Rub a warm, moist towel along the bottom of each tray for a few minutes. Then carefully slide a small rubber spatula between each eyeball and the edge of its holder and pop the eyeball out. Repeat with the remaining eyeballs and arrange them on your serving platter.

7. Press one black jellybean into the center of each colored iris. Refrigerate uneaten eyes.

Makes: 2 dozen eyesores

Potato Bug Bits

Begin an exciting career as an insect exterminator today! You can start with one of the biggest and ugliest beetles of all—the potato bug.

INGREDIENTS

6-ounce package barbecue-flavored potato chips
1 cup margarine
4 medium baking potatoes
32 pieces large puffed corn
12-ounce bag chow mein noodles

Microwave/Stove Top and Oven

TOOLS YOU'LL NEED

- large reclosable plastic bag
- rolling pin
- small mixing bowl
- microwave-safe bowl
- pot holders
- paper towels
- cutting board
- utility knife
- 13- by 9- by 2-inch baking dish
- fork
- toothpick

1. Pour the potato chips into the reclosable bag, remove as much air as you can, and seal the bag. Place the bag on your work surface, and firmly roll the rolling pin over the chips to crush them thoroughly. Pour the crushed chips into a small mixing bowl and set aside.

2. Put the margarine into a microwave-safe bowl and heat on high (100%) for about 40 seconds or until the margarine has melted. Use the pot holders and ask an adult to help you remove the bowl from the microwave. Set aside to cool slightly. (Margarine may also be melted in a small saucepan over low heat with an adult's help.)

3. With an adult's help, preheat oven to 350 degrees. Wash your potatoes and pat them lightly to dry with a paper towel. Place them on a cutting board and ask an adult to help you cut each potato lengthwise, with a utility knife, into eight equal, finger-shaped wedges.

4. Make an assembly line on your work surface consisting of potato wedges, bowl of melted butter, bowl of crushed chips, and 13- by 9- by 2-inch baking dish. To make potato bug body, dip one wedge completely in the margarine. Place it into the bowl of chips and turn it over to coat both sides of potato wedge. Remove the potato bug from the bowl and lay it inside the baking dish. Repeat with remaining ingredients. Arrange potato bugs in dish about $\frac{1}{2}$ inch apart.

5. With an adult's help, place the dish in the oven and bake for about 20 minutes. Then, using a fork and pot holders, carefully turn over each potato bug to brown the other side. Continue baking for 20 more minutes or until the potato bugs are soft in the center. Remove from the oven and let potato bugs stand until they are cool enough for you to handle.

6. To make heads, poke two holes into each piece of puffed corn using a toothpick, then insert two chow mein noodles into each piece of puffed corn so that the noodles extend equally on each side.

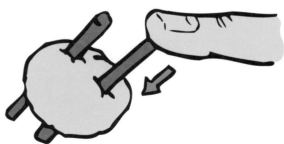

7. Poke three chow mein noodles into the side of each potato bug body so that the noodles are equal on each side. This will form six legs per bug. Then carefully press one head into each potato bug so that the noodles stick out on one side and poke directly into the potato bug body on the other. Serve immediately. You can prepare potato bug heads up to one day ahead and store them in a tightly sealed container. Potato bug bodies can be made up to three hours in advance and stored, tightly covered, in the refrigerator. Just before serving, reheat them in the microwave on high (100%) for two to three minutes.

Serves: 8 bugged buddies (4 bugs a piece)

Putrid Presentation
Assemble bugs on individual plates lying on their backs as if they've died in agony. Pour about 1 tablespoon barbecue sauce to serve as the bug's fresh and oozing blood.

Sickening Sweets

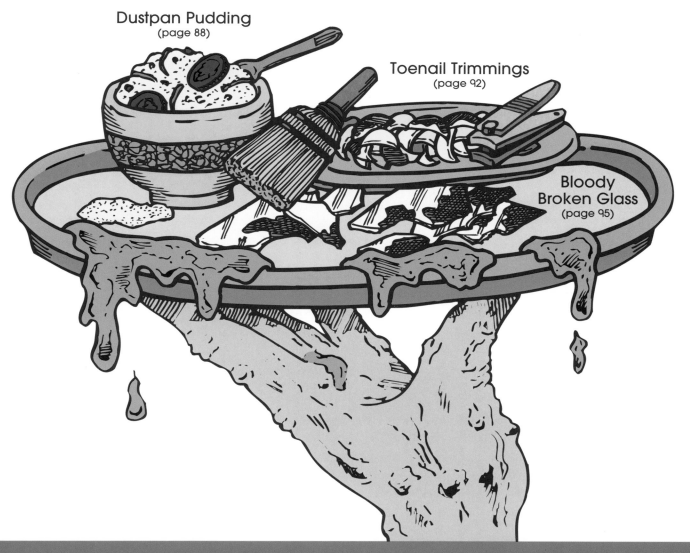

Dustpan Pudding
(page 88)

Toenail Trimmings
(page 92)

Bloody Broken Glass
(page 95)

Outhouse Delight

Here's one nasty pile of dessert tasty enough to feed the whole gang!

INGREDIENTS

6 ounces white chocolate chips

$\frac{1}{4}$ cup light corn syrup

5. l-ounce package chocolate-flavored instant pudding and pie filling mix

1 quart milk (not 3 cups as directed in the pudding box), well chilled

16-ounce can ready made German chocolate cake frosting

12 dark chocolate cookies, broken into chunks

Stove Top

TOOLS YOU'LL NEED

- double boiler
- rubber spatula
- small mixing bowl
- plastic wrap
- waxed paper
- rolling pin
- ruler
- utility knife
- large mixing bowl
- whisk
- ladle
- soup bowls

1. The toilet tissue dough requires several hours to fully set, so you may wish to make this recipe at least one day in advance. Fill the lower portion of your double boiler with water. With an adult's help, heat the water over medium heat. In the upper portion of the boiler, add the white chocolate chips and corn syrup.

2. Stir constantly with a rubber spatula until mixture is smooth. Remove from heat and carefully pour the chocolate mixture into a small mixing bowl. Set it aside to cool to room temperature. Cover with plastic wrap *directly touching* your chocolate toilet tissue dough, and let it stand until the mixture becomes shiny and doughy.

3. After the dough has set, place it onto your work surface between two sheets of waxed paper, and press the dough into a disc. Use a rolling pin to flatten the dough to an $\frac{1}{8}$-inch thickness. Then pull off the top layer of waxed paper to prevent it from sticking to the tissue mixture.

4. Using your ruler and utility knife, have an adult help you cut the dough into eight 2-inch squares of toilet tissue. Turn dough over on your work surface and remove the lower layer of waxed paper. With clean, dry hands, gently crumple the individual squares to create a realistic-looking toilet tissue wad. Set them aside, tightly covered with plastic wrap, at room temperature.

5. Pour the instant chocolate pudding mix and the milk into a large mixing bowl, and whisk vigorously for two minutes to blend the ingredients thoroughly. Scoop the German chocolate frosting into the pudding mixture by rounded teaspoonfuls. Pour in the crushed cookies and fold together lightly with the spatula to create a wonderfully lumpy outhouse dump mixture.

6. Ladle dump mixture into soup bowls. Place one ball of crumpled toilet paper in the center of each bowl and serve immediately. You can prepare the dough (steps 1 and 2 only) up to three days in advance and store it, covered, at room temperature. Then roll it out and crumple it a few hours before serving. Outhouse Delight is most natural looking and runny when prepared just before serving. Store leftovers in the refrigerator.

Makes: 8 bowls of soupy poopies

Dustpan Pudding

If people have ever told you not to eat off the floor, they have no idea what they're missing. This pile of dirt is downright delicious!

INGREDIENTS

$\frac{3}{4}$ cup any type light-colored crunchy sugar cookie*
$\frac{3}{4}$ cup graham crackers*
1 cup any type dark chocolate crunchy cookie*
2 packages (3.5 to 4 ounces each) vanilla-flavored instant pudding and pie filling mix
4 cups milk
8-ounce container nondairy whipped topping
1 box (10$\frac{1}{2}$ ounces) miniature chocolate chip cookies
16 snips of shoelace licorice (of varied lengths from 1 to 3 inches), any color
8 to 10 gold-foil-wrapped coins, foils removed
candy rocks (realistic candy rocks, available at candy shops and many supermarkets)

*To measure cookies properly, crush them slightly before filling the measuring cup.

TOOLS YOU'LL NEED

- food processor, fitted with metal chopping blade
- large mixing bowl
- mixing spoon
- whisk
- rubber spatula
- 2$\frac{1}{2}$-quart serving bowl
- plastic wrap

1. Ask an adult to help you pour the crushed sugar cookies, graham crackers, and dark chocolate cookies into a food processor. Thoroughly blend until crumbs are the consistency of granulated sugar. Set aside. (If you do not have a food processor, place all three cookie types into a reclosable plastic bag, remove excess air, and seal. Crush thoroughly with a rolling pin.)

2. In a large mixing bowl, prepare both pudding mixes and milk according to package direction. Use a whisk to mix thoroughly.

3. With a rubber spatula, fold in the whipped topping and chocolate chip cookies.

4. To assemble, spoon half of the pudding mixture into a serving bowl. Then sprinkle with half of the cookie dust. Repeat with a second layer of each. Cover with plastic wrap and refrigerate for at least four hours. This portion can be prepared up to one day in advance. Just before serving your dust pile, decorate with things you've "swept off the floor": licorice snips as thread, chocolate coins, and candy rocks. Be sure guests get at least one rock and a piece of thread on their dust pile.

Serves: 16 dust bunnies

Putrid Presentation

*Ask an adult to buy you a new dustpan to use **only** when you're serving this delicious dessert. Serve guests their pudding in individual bowls. Then, using a clean pastry brush, dust off the decorative thread, rocks, and coins into each guests bowl. What a great way to dispose of your dirt!*

Feces Pieces

These bite-sized bits of thick, pasty poops look like they took loads of effort—but you can put these together in no time!

INGREDIENTS

$\frac{3}{4}$ cup chunk peanut butter
$\frac{1}{4}$ cup unsweetened cocoa
$\frac{1}{4}$ cup butter or margarine, softened
1 cup flaked coconut
$\frac{1}{2}$ cup finely chopped walnuts
$\frac{1}{2}$ cup corn, frozen, thawed, and drained
2 to $2\frac{1}{2}$ cups confectioners' sugar, divided

TOOLS YOU'LL NEED

- baking sheet
- waxed paper
- large mixing bowl
- electric mixer
- cutting board or marble pastry board
- plastic wrap

1. Line baking sheet with waxed paper and set aside. Clear a spot in the refrigerator big enough to fit the baking sheet.

2. Place the peanut butter, unsweetened cocoa, and butter or margarine into a mixing bowl. Ask an adult to help you use the electric mixer to mix thoroughly until creamed.

3. Add in the coconut, walnuts, corn, and 1 cup confectioners' sugar. Mix on lowest speed until blended well.

4. Sprinkle some of the remaining sugar onto your cutting board or marble pastry board. Place the peanut butter mixture onto the board and knead in 1 cup confectioners' sugar with your clean, dry hands. Continue kneading until it's thoroughly blended. The mixture should hold its shape easily when formed. If it is not firm enough, add additional powdered sugar a tablespoon at a time.

5. To shape feces, scoop one rounded tablespoonful into your hands and roll into a poop shape. Place on the paper-lined baking sheet. Repeat with remaining dough. Each poop is unique, so shape each one differently.

6. Cover Feces Pieces with plastic wrap and place in the refrigerator for one hour to harden them. These satisfying bowel movements can be made up to one week in advance and stored in the refrigerator, covered tightly.

Makes: 2 dozen little stinkers

Freaky Fact
Though nobody on record has ever died of constipation, there have been some mighty long cases of bathroom absenteeism—many over one year! That could add up to anywhere from 60 to 100 pounds of excess poop—not to mention a great deal of discomfort!

Toenail Trimmings

A delectable treat for all the nail-biters on your guest list. Toenail trimmings are a truly habit-forming delicacy!

INGREDIENTS

1 $\frac{1}{2}$ cups confectioners' sugar
1 cup butter, softened
1 egg
1 $\frac{1}{2}$ teaspoons vanilla extract
2 $\frac{3}{4}$ cups all-purpose flour, divided
1 teaspoon baking soda
1 teaspoon cream of tartar

For nail polish:
2 cups confectioners' sugar
$\frac{1}{4}$ cup light corn syrup
2 tablespoons water
red and orange food coloring
blue food coloring (optional)

Oven

TOOLS YOU'LL NEED

- large mixing bowl
- electric mixer
- plastic wrap
- rolling pin
- ruler
- flat saucer
- 3 different-sized round cookie cutters or round plastic-container lids
- baking sheet, greased
- pot holders
- flat metal spatula
- wire rack
- medium mixing bowl
- whisk
- 3 small mixing bowls
- small rubber spatula

1. Combine confectioners' sugar, butter, egg, vanilla, 2 $\frac{1}{4}$ cups flour, baking soda, and cream of tartar into a large mixing bowl. Ask an adult to help you use the electric mixer to blend ingredients first on low speed, then on medium, until thoroughly blended. Remove dough from mixing bowl and cover tightly in plastic wrap. Chill dough in the refrigerator for two or three hours or overnight.

2. When the dough has chilled, ask an adult to help you preheat the oven to 375 degrees. With some of the remaining flour, lightly flour your work surface and rolling pin. Remove one-third of the dough from the refrigerator and roll it to $\frac{1}{4}$-inch thickness.

3. Place about $\frac{1}{4}$ cup of the remaining flour into a flat saucer to be used for flouring toenail cookie cutters. To cut toenails, dip each cookie cutter or plastic lid into the flour to coat it lightly. Starting at the edge of the dough, cut out thin crescent shapes. Lay the toenails onto a greased baking sheet. Each toenail should be about $\frac{3}{4}$-inch to 1-inch wide at the center of the toenail. Length of clippings will vary with the size of the cookie cutter. Repeat with remaining dough. Note: Baking time will be less for small toenails and more for large ones, so bake sizes separately.

4. Use pot holders and ask an adult to help you place the greased baking sheet into the oven. Bake for five minutes to seven minutes or until lightly browned. Have an adult help you remove the toenails from the oven and let them set for a minute. Use a flat metal spatula to transfer them to a wire rack to cool completely.

5. To prepare nail polish, place the confectioners' sugar, corn syrup, and water into a medium mixing bowl. Blend thoroughly with your whisk until all sugar lumps are dissolved. Divide mixture evenly into three small mixing bowls. Add a few drops of red food coloring to one bowl to create red nail polish and a few drops of orange food coloring to another bowl to create orange nail polish. Leave the remaining bowl uncolored for a white polish, or add a few drops of blue to this last bowl for a hot new high-fashion shade.

6. While they are still on the rack, polish the nail clippings using a small rubber spatula.

7. Allow clippings to sit on the racks overnight for the polish to harden. You can prepare toenail clippings up to two months in advance. Store them in an airtight reclosable bag and freeze them for later use.

Makes: About 6 dozen toenail trimming treats

Freaky Fact

Fingernails grow at a rate of about 0.02 inches a week—that's about four times faster than toenails. So, cherish these crunchy toenails—they've taken a long time to prepare!

Bloody Broken Glass

This dessert is truly a cut above the rest!

INGREDIENTS

1 cup light corn syrup
1 cup water
2 cups sugar
½ teaspoon clear-colored candy flavoring oil (such as lemon or peppermint)
6 ounces red confectionery coating

Stove Top

TOOLS YOU'LL NEED

- nonstick baking sheet with a raised edge, or a lightly greased baking sheet
- large, heavy saucepan with lid
- wooden spoon
- pot holders
- candy thermometer
- waxed paper
- double boiler
- whisk

1. Place the baking sheet in the refrigerator to chill.

2. Pour the corn syrup, water, and sugar into a heavy saucepan. Ask an adult to help you heat the mixture over medium-high heat. Use a wooden spoon to stir constantly until sugar dissolves.

3. Bring the mixture to a boil. Cover the pan and continue boiling for about three minutes so steam can melt any sugar crystals that have built up on the sides of the saucepan.

4. Remove the lid using pot holders. Be sure to have an adult help you. Place the candy thermometer into the sugar mixture, and rest it on or clip it to the side of the saucepan. Continue to cook the mixture, uncovered, without stirring, over high heat until the thermometer reads 310 degrees or "hard crack" stage.

5. Remove pan from heat and place it on a pot holder on your work surface. Allow it to cool to 160 degrees. Then stir in the candy flavoring oil with the wooden spoon.

6. Remove the baking sheet from the refrigerator and place it on your work surface. With your hands protected by pot holders, hold the chilled baking sheet and have an adult pour the candy mixture onto the baking sheet. Quickly tip the baking sheet back and forth to spread the hot sugar mixture as evenly and thinly as possible to create clear "glass." (Do not attempt to scrape the cooking pan to remove excess sugar mixture. Instead place the pan under hot water to dissolve the sugar and wash out the pan.) Return the baking sheet to the refrigerator.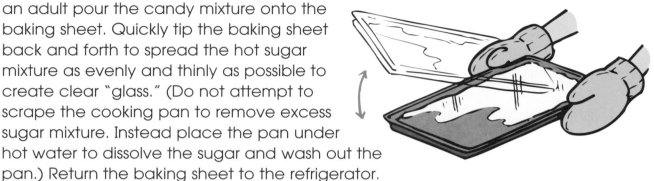

7. When the candy glass has hardened, lay waxed paper down on your work surface. Crack the candy into pieces of all shapes and sizes and set them on the waxed paper.

8. Fill the lower portion of a double boiler half full with water. With an adult's help, place the double boiler on the stove and turn the burner on medium heat. When the water begins to simmer, pour the confectionery coating into the upper portion. Stir occasionally with a whisk while the coating melts.

9. With an adult's help, turn the heat to lowest possible setting to prevent coating from thickening. Place a length of waxed paper on a suitable work surface close to the double boiler.

10. Quickly dip the tips of a piece of broken glass into the melted "blood" and hold it upright so that drips form as the coating hardens. Place it on the waxed paper to cool and set. Repeat with the remaining pieces of glass. You can prepare Bloody Broken Glass up to two weeks in advance. Put waxed paper between each layer of the glass and store in a tightly sealed container lined with waxed paper.

Makes: About 1 ¾ pounds shattered shards

Putrid Presentation

Add variety to your bloody accident by coloring the glass in popular bottle colors, such as brown or green. Simply add a few drops of green food coloring, or equal parts red and green to make a classic root beer-bottle brown.

Cryonic Creeps

You'll just die over these chilly bodies! They're frozen for science—and for you and your friends to enjoy anytime.

INGREDIENTS

4 eggs
1 $\frac{1}{4}$ cups sugar
$\frac{1}{8}$ teaspoon salt
$\frac{1}{3}$ cup cornstarch
4 cups milk
14-ounce can sweetened condensed milk
2 tablespoons vanilla extract
16 small candy eyes or any small, round candies
1 cup popped corn

Stove Top

TOOLS YOU'LL NEED

* medium mixing bowl
* whisk
* large, heavy saucepan
* wooden spoon
* pot holders
* can opener
* plastic wrap
* serving plates
* 8 gingerbread man molds (available at craft and baking supply stores)

1. Beat the eggs in a medium mixing bowl with a whisk. Gradually add the sugar, salt, and cornstarch. Continue beating until thoroughly blended. Set aside.

2. Pour the milk into a large, heavy saucepan. Ask an adult to help you bring the milk to a boil, stirring constantly with a wooden spoon to prevent it from burning.

3. Using pot holders, have an adult pour about $\frac{1}{4}$ cup hot milk into the egg mixture. Mix lightly with your whisk, then pour the mixture into the saucepan. This process prevents the egg mixture from clumping.

4. Continue cooking the mixture, stirring constantly with the wooden spoon for six to eight minutes or until mixture thickens and coats the spoon. Open the sweetened condensed milk with a can opener. Gradually stir in the canned milk and vanilla and mix well. Remove the saucepan from your stove top and place on a heat-safe work surface.

5. Allow the custard mixture to cool, then cover the saucepan with plastic wrap and place it in the refrigerator for three to four hours.

6. Meanwhile, line your gingerbread man molds with plastic wrap, pressing the plastic wrap into the mold's crevices. Be sure to leave enough plastic hanging over the sides so that you can grab on to it when you're ready to unmold the men. Fill each mold about three-quarters full with custard mixture. Cover each mold with plastic wrap and place it in the freezer for three to four hours or overnight to harden.

7. To serve, let Cryonic Creeps stand at room temperature for about five minutes. Then unmold each treat onto individual serving plates and carefully peel away its plastic wrap. Decorate each person with two individual candy eyes and popped corn for bushy hair. Serve immediately. You can freeze these dead guys up to one week in advance and unmold as directed. Decorate just before serving.

Makes: 8 cool cadavers

Amputated Tongues

Tongues will be a waggin' over these easy-to-make delectable desserts!

INGREDIENTS

1 pound pink confectionery coating
16-ounce package peanut-shaped peanut butter cookies
white nonpareils

Stove Top
TOOLS YOU'LL NEED

- double boiler
- pot holders
- whisk
- waxed paper
- tongs
- small rubber spatula

1. Fill the lower portion of the double boiler halfway with water. With an adult's help, place the double boiler on the stove and turn the burner on medium heat. When the water begins to simmer, pour the confectionery coating into the upper portion. Stir occasionally with a whisk while coating melts.

2. With an adult's help, turn heat to lowest possible setting to prevent coating from thickening. Place a length of waxed paper on a suitable work surface close to the double boiler.

3. To assemble tongues, ask an adult to hold the pan with pot holders while you dip the cookies. Using tongs, pick up one cookie and completely dip it into the melted pink coating. Lift it up, allowing excess coating to drip off, and place it onto the waxed paper. Immediately sprinkle white nonpareils lightly over the tongue to make taste buds. Repeat with the remaining cookies.

4. To cover the uncoated areas on the tongues left by the tongs, dip a small rubber spatula into the melted pink coating and spread it over the uncovered portion. Allow the cookies to cool completely. Store the tongues, covered, at room temperature for up to three days, or frozen, in a tightly sealed container, for up to two months.

Makes: About 3 dozen tasty tongues

Putrid Presentation

Hairy tongue is a strange but real malady in which a person's tongue actually appears to grow hair! Why not create an entire batch of wonderfully hairy tongues to tempt the whole gang? Add black food coloring to $\frac{1}{2}$ cup shredded coconut. Then, instead of the white nonpareils, sprinkle the black coconut over the tops of the freshly dipped tongues.

Hairballs

Enjoy this hairy delicacy when your cat is shedding its fur. They certainly taste better than the real thing!

INGREDIENTS

1 roll ready-made chocolate cookie dough (with nuts or chips, optional)
7-ounce bag sweetened shredded coconut
black, orange, or brown food coloring (the color of your kitty's fur)
16-ounce can ready-to-spread chocolate frosting

Oven

TOOLS YOU'LL NEED

- butter knife
- baking sheet, lightly greased
- pot holders
- metal spatula
- wire racks
- small mixing bowl
- fork
- small rubber spatula

1. With a butter knife, cut the dough log into 12 even slices. (Each slice should equal about 2 generous tablespoons.)

2. To shape hairballs, roll a section of dough between your clean, dry hands into a tube shape about $\frac{1}{2}$ inch by 2 inches. Repeat with remaining dough. Arrange cookies about 2 inches apart on lightly greased baking sheet.

3. With an adult's help, preheat oven to 350 degrees. Place baking sheet in freezer and chill for about 15 minutes or until dough is firm.

4. Ask an adult to help you remove the hairballs from the freezer and place them in the oven. Bake about 15 minutes or until set. Using pot holders, have an adult help you remove them from the oven.

5. With an adult's help, use a metal spatula to remove the cookies from the baking sheet and place them on wire racks to cool. Pour the shredded coconut into a small mixing bowl and add food coloring of your choice, drop by drop, until you've matched your kitty's coat color. Mix thoroughly with a fork to distribute the food coloring.

6. When cookies have cooled completely, spread the tops and sides of each cookie with chocolate frosting using a rubber spatula. Then roll each hairball in the coconut, pressing with your hands to help the coconut stick to the hairball. Allow hairballs to air dry for two to three hours or overnight before serving. After drying, hairballs can be served immediately or frozen for up to two months in a tightly sealed container. Do not overlap hairballs when storing, and be sure to put waxed paper between layers.

Makes: 12 clumps of kitty coat

Freaky Fact

The largest recorded domestic cat was a male tabby named Himmy, owned by Thomas Vyse of Redlynch, Queensland, Australia. Himmy weighed in at a whopping 46 pounds, 15¼ ounces and had a massive 33-inch waistline! One can only wonder . . . do big cats make big hairballs?

Doggie-Drop Cookies

Move over, Rover. These doggie leftovers are worth a second bite!

INGREDIENTS

1 $\frac{1}{2}$ cups semi-sweet chocolate chips
$\frac{1}{2}$ cup chunky peanut butter
2 tablespoons butter or margarine
36 large marshmallows

Microwave/Stove Top

TOOLS YOU'LL NEED

- baking sheet
- waxed paper
- large microwave-safe bowl
- plastic wrap
- pot holders
- rubber spatula
- metal spatula
- serving plates

1. Clear a space in the refrigerator large enough for a baking sheet. Line the baking sheet with waxed paper and set aside.

2. Pour the semi-sweet chocolate chips, peanut butter, and butter or margarine into a large microwave-safe bowl. Cover lightly with plastic wrap. With an adult's help, microwave on high (100%) for about one and a half minutes. Use pot holders to remove bowl from microwave. Stir well with a rubber spatula. Cover and return to the microwave. Cook on high for approximately one and a half minutes longer and stir again. Repeat until chocolate chips are smooth and melted. (This step may also be done with an adult's help using a double boiler on the stove.)

3. Allow the chocolate mixture to cool slightly, about two to three minutes. Fold in the marshmallows and stir with the rubber spatula to coat completely with the chocolate mixture.

4. When the chocolate mixture has cooled enough for you to handle with your clean, dry hands, remove marshmallows from chocolate mixture and arrange them in sets of three on your baking sheet. Keeping marshmallows close together, form random doggie-poop shapes.

5. Drizzle the remaining chocolate mixture evenly over each doggie dropping. Note: If excess chocolate mixture spreads too far from the poop, use the rubber spatula to push it back into shape.

6. Chill for about an hour (or until firm) in the refrigerator. Store doggie droppings, covered, in the refrigerator for up to three days. These can be made ahead and frozen, tightly covered, for up to two months. Just before serving, carefully lift the droppings from the lined baking sheet using a metal spatula and transfer them to individual serving plates. Serve with forks so guests can scoop their plates clean plop by plop.

Makes: 12 doggie dinners

SNIFF!!
SNIFF!!

Putrid Presentation
Large marshmallows will produce German shepherd-sized doggie dung, but you can serve up a batch of poodle-sized poops, too, by using mini marshmallows instead. You'll need about 3 cups mini marshmallows.

Kitty Litter Clumps

They're stinkin' good!

INGREDIENTS

4 medium-sized bananas
3 cups peanuts or walnuts
1 cup chunky peanut butter
6 ounces dark chocolate confectionery coating
blue jimmie sprinkles

Microwave/Stove Top
TOOLS YOU'LL NEED

- utility knife
- food processor fitted with metal chopping blade
- 13- by 9- by 2-inch baking dish
- large microwave-safe bowl
- plastic wrap
- pot holders
- rubber spatula
- tongs

1. With an adult's help, use a utility knife to cut each banana in half widthwise, then lengthwise. You will have 16 finger-shaped banana wedges. Set them aside.

2. With an adult's help, pour the peanuts or walnuts into the food processor. Chop nuts into kitty litter-sized chunks similar to rough sand. Spread the nuts into 13- by 9- by 2-inch baking dish and set aside.

3. Place the chunky peanut butter and dark chocolate confectionery coating into a microwave-safe bowl. Cover lightly with plastic wrap. With an adult's help, microwave on high (100%) for about one minute. Use pot holders to remove bowl from microwave. Stir well with a rubber spatula. Cover and return to microwave. Cook on high for approximately one more minute and stir again. Repeat until chocolate chunks are completely melted. Use pot holders to place the bowl on your work surface. (The peanut butter and chocolate may also be melted with an adult's help using a double boiler.)

4. To create kitty clumps, begin completely coating the banana chunks by dipping them into the melted chocolate mixture with tongs. You'll want to do this step quickly. Lay them on the bed of chopped nuts and roll them with tongs so that all sides are coated. Then liberally sprinkle all sides with blue jimmies to create flecks of colored deodorizing crystals that keep the stench away—almost!

5. Move the kitty litter clumps off to one side while you continue coating the remaining bananas. Leave excess jimmies or crystals mixed in with the nuts as you continue coating bananas. Before serving, bury some of the cat poops in the remaining nuts, as any polite cat would, and lightly sprinkle additional jimmies or crystals over entire tray. Cover lightly and store in the refrigerator. Kitty Litter Clumps can be made two to three hours in advance, or covered tightly and frozen up to two weeks in advance. If you freeze them, move the tray to the refrigerator 20 minutes before serving. Do not refreeze.

Makes: 16 fancy feline feces

Morbid Munchies

Brain Cell Salad
(page 121)

Handwiches
(page 123)

Bad Breath Biscuits
(page 127)

Cellulite Salad

Straight from your plastic surgeon's "waist" basket, this fatty, lumpy, clumpy salad makes a delicious side dish!

INGREDIENTS

14-ounce can sweetened condensed milk
$\frac{1}{4}$ cup lemon juice
20-ounce can crushed pineapple, drained
16-ounce can whole-berry cranberry sauce
red food coloring
2 cups mini marshmallows
2 cups large marshmallows
8-ounce container ready-made whipped topping
$\frac{1}{2}$ cup raspberry preserves

TOOLS YOU'LL NEED

- large mixing bowl
- whisk
- medium mixing bowl
- rubber spatula
- 13- by 9- by 2-inch baking dish
- plastic wrap
- serving plates

1. In a large mixing bowl, combine the sweetened condensed milk and lemon juice, and blend thoroughly with a whisk. Set aside.

2. Stir the pineapple and cranberry sauce together in a medium mixing bowl. Add five to seven drops of red food coloring and blend well with a rubber spatula. Set aside for five to ten minutes or until pineapple takes on a dark red color. Add more food coloring if necessary.

3. Fold the pineapple-cranberry mixture (blood and blood clots) into the milk mixture. Fold in all the marshmallows (cellulite clumps) and toss until the marshmallows are lightly coated with the clotted blood mixture. Finally, lightly fold in the ready-made whipped topping so that the mixture is not completely blended. It should appear marbleized. DO NOT over mix.

4. Spoon the cellulite mixture into a 13- by 9- by 2-inch baking dish. Use a tablespoon to scoop up dollops of raspberry preserves (clots of thickened blood). Hold each scoop about 12 inches above the cellulite salad, and allow it to drop and splatter onto the salad.

5. Cover tightly with plastic wrap and freeze until firm, about four hours or overnight. Allow cellulite to sit at room temperature for about 10 minutes before scooping it onto individual serving plates. May be prepared up to one week in advance and stored, tightly covered, in the freezer.

Serves: 12 to 16 blubber lovers

Putrid Presentation

Did that sloppy plastic surgeon suck up some veins along with the cellulite? Fold several pieces of red or black shoelace licorice into the salad. Leave some veins buried in the cellulite and hang pieces over the sides like wiggling arteries.

Taxidermist's Leftovers

Taxidermy, the art of stuffing dead animals for display, is a job with added benefits! Entrails, bones, and unidentifiable body parts blend together for this light and yummy side dish. It's especially delicious when you're feeling a little "stuffed."

INGREDIENTS

4 cups fresh or frozen cranberries
$\frac{1}{4}$ cup water
8 baking apples
1 pear
2 small bananas
1 cup sugar

Stove Top

TOOLS YOU'LL NEED

- large, heavy saucepan with lid
- vegetable peeler and corer
- paring knife
- sieve
- fork
- wooden spoon
- large serving bowl
- plastic wrap

1. Place the cranberries and water into a heavy saucepan. With an adult's help, place the saucepan over burner and simmer for 20 to 25 minutes or until tender. Set aside to cool at room temperature.

2. Have an adult help you peel the apples and pear with the vegetable peeler. With the paring knife, cut the pear in half lengthwise and remove the seeds. Cut four of the peeled apples into eight finger-shaped wedges and remove the seeds. Cut the fifth apple in half widthwise and the sixth apple in half lengthwise. Remove seeds. Core the remaining two apples, which means remove the seeds and leave the apples whole. Peel the bananas and cut one in half widthwise, and the other one in half lengthwise, then widthwise. Now your taxidermy pieces are in a wide variety of unidentifiable body shapes. Set these body parts aside.

3. When the cranberries have cooled, press them with your clean hands through a sieve to extract the juice. Collect the juice in the saucepan. Discard skins and pulp.

4. Add all the apples and pear pieces to the cranberry juice. With an adult's help, place the saucepan over burner and simmer, covered, for about 30 minutes. Add the bananas and continue simmering for 10 to 15 minutes or until the whole apples are tender. To test, stick a fork into an apple—it should glide in easily. Add the sugar and gently stir with a wooden spoon to coat fruit in the sauce. The bananas will break apart slightly and give the appearance of membrane and cartilage. Simmer for five more minutes, stirring occasionally. Transfer to a large serving bowl and chill, tightly covered with plastic wrap, in the refrigerator until you're ready to serve. Taxidermist's Leftovers can be made up to two days in advance.

Serves: 8 to 10 boneless buddies

Putrid Presentation
Get guests into a "wild" mood! Create an animal-pelt placemat for each guest out of squares of fake fur (available at fabric supply stores).

Rotten Eggs

If you're scrambling for a last-minute side dish, whip up some of these rotten-egg look-alikes. These fruit-and-custard egg imposters appear to be massively moldy sunny-side-up eggs.

INGREDIENTS

1 cup ready-made whipped topping
green food coloring
5.1-ounce package instant vanilla-flavored pudding and pie filling mix
3½ cups cold milk
16-ounce can peach halves, drained

TOOLS YOU'LL NEED

- small mixing bowl
- whisk
- large mixing bowl
- dessert plates

1. Place the ready-made whipped topping into a small mixing bowl. Add two or three drops of green food coloring and blend well with a whisk to create a light green shade of mold. Be careful not to over stir. Set aside.

2. Pour the instant vanilla pudding mix and milk into a large mixing bowl. (Note: This is slightly more milk than suggested in the directions on the pudding box, but these rotten eggs are supposed to be a bit runny and undercooked!) To blend ingredients, whisk for about two minutes, then pour at once into individual dessert plates, dividing evenly. This will be the white portion of the rotten eggs.

3. Arrange one peach half in the center of each egg white. To add rotten mold to your sunny-side-up eggs, scoop out one rounded teaspoonful of the green whipped-topping mixture. Hold it high above one of the eggs and allow it to drop and splatter on the egg. Repeat one or two more times.

4. Splatter the rest of the dessert plates with the greenish mixture. Place the plates in the refrigerator for about 15 minutes before serving. You can prepare the mold and rotten-egg whites in advance. Cover tightly with plastic wrap and store in the refrigerator up to a day ahead. Then, before serving, do steps 3 and 4.

Serves: 6 egg-centric friends

Putrid Presentation
Toss a small handful of "cracked eggshells" (hardened mini marshmallows) in for added texture!

Maggot Man

This larvae-infested freak is sure to turn some heads at your next potluck!

INGREDIENTS

2 tablespoons butter or margarine
½ cup chopped onion
2 cups uncooked long-grain white rice
4 cups chicken or vegetable broth
1 tablespoon dried parsley flakes
2 teaspoons dried basil
1 teaspoon poultry seasoning
½ teaspoon salt
½ teaspoon pepper
¾ cup grated Jack cheese

For decorating:
2 cauliflower florets*
1 circular slice from a green bell pepper, cut in half*
1 circular slice from a red bell pepper end (the bumpy bottom), cut in half*
1 baby carrot
ice cubes
3 leaves fresh kale
2 peas
1 cherry tomato
2 slices black olive

*Save remaining portions of vegetables for your next meal, or chop them up and stir-fry with a few tablespoons oil as a separate side dish.

Stove Top

TOOLS YOU'LL NEED

- large, covered saucepan
- wooden spoon
- 6-cup capacity round serving bowl
- plastic wrap
- medium saucepan
- colander
- pot holders
- round serving platter, about 2 inches larger around than your serving bowl

1. To prepare the maggot filling, place the butter or margarine and onion in a large saucepan. With an adult's help, place saucepan on a burner and melt butter over medium heat. Cook onion until soft. Use a wooden spoon to stir in the rice, broth, parsley, basil, poultry seasoning, salt, and pepper. Bring mixture to a boil. Cover saucepan and reduce heat to low. Simmer 20 to 25 minutes or until rice is tender.

2. While the rice is simmering, line a round serving bowl with plastic wrap. Set aside.

3. Fill a medium saucepan halfway with water. With an adult's help, bring water to a boil over high heat. Add the cauliflower, green, and red bell peppers, and carrot. Boil for three minutes to soften the vegetables. Get an adult to help you pour the boiling water and vegetables into a colander to drain. (Be sure to use pot holders.) Refill the saucepan with water and ice cubes. Return vegetables to saucepan to stop the cooking process. Set aside.

4. When the rice mixture is done, remove the large saucepan from heat with an adult's help, and stir in the cheese using the wooden spoon. Spoon mixture into the serving bowl lined with plastic wrap. Cover the top with more plastic wrap and press down firmly to mold rice mixture onto the shape of the bowl—Maggot Man's head. Remove the top layer of plastic wrap and let stand for 10 minutes.

5. To assemble Maggot Man's head, place the kale leaves close together around the rim of the serving platter. The leaves will be his wild bushy hairdo. With an adult's help, invert the bowl onto the platter over the kale. Gently pat the bottom of the bowl to loosen the rice. Remove bowl, leaving the plastic wrap over the maggot filling. With your hands over the plastic wrap, shape the filling into an oval by gently but firmly pressing in on the sides. Remove plastic wrap and discard.

6. Create Maggot Man's facial features using the cooked vegetables as follows:
   - eyes: cauliflower florets, with a pea on top of each
   - nose: cherry tomato
   - eyebrows: break each olive slice and pull it into a semi-straight line
   - ears: a green bell pepper slice on each side
   - mouth: carrot placed vertically for an undulating uvula, and red bell pepper slices for upper and lower lips

Note: Maggot filling can be made up to three days ahead of time. Follow steps 1 through 4 and refrigerate, tightly covered, until you're ready to serve. At that time, microwave on high (100%) for three to four minutes. Decorate as directed in steps 5 and 6 and serve.

Makes: 10 to 12 maggot munchers

Putrid Presentation
*Set the mood for all your fly larvae-loving buddies and pop the cult classic **The Fly** into the VCR after dinner.*

Bowel Bundles

No human waste here! Every bowl will be a tidy one when you're serving this entrail treat.

INGREDIENTS

4 cups all-purpose flour, divided plus extra for kneading
2 packages instant yeast
$\frac{1}{2}$ teaspoon salt
$\frac{1}{2}$ cup very warm (not boiling) water
2 tablespoons olive oil
6 foot-long hot dogs

Oven

TOOLS YOU'LL NEED

- large mixing bowl
- whisk
- dish towel
- utility knife
- rolling pin
- ruler
- baking sheet, greased and floured
- pot holders

1. In a large mixing bowl, combine 2 cups flour with the yeast and salt. Use a whisk to gently stir ingredients. Pour the very warm water and olive oil into the dry ingredients and continue stirring until a sticky batter is formed.

2. Slowly add the remaining flour and mix together with your clean, dry hands until it forms a moist (but not sticky) ball of dough.

3. Sprinkle flour lightly over your work surface and place the dough in the center. Using the palms of your hands, knead the dough for about six minutes or until the dough is smooth. Do not overknead, as dough will become chewy. Return dough to the large mixing bowl and cover it with a dry dish towel. Place bowl in a warm, dry place for 10 minutes.

4. While you're waiting, ask an adult to help you preheat the oven to 475 degrees. Then, using your utility knife, cut slices into the hot dogs. The slices should go about three-fourths of the way into each hot dog widthwise, about 1 inch apart. This will allow the hot dog "bowels" to be easily bent and twisted after covering them in dough. Be careful no to cut all the way through the hot dogs. Set them aside.

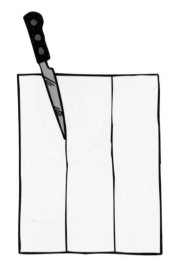

5. Divide the dough into two balls and set one aside. Place the other ball of dough on a lightly floured surface and gently pat it flat with your hands. Then rub flour on a rolling pin and roll if back and forth over the dough. Shape it into a 9- by 12-inch rectangle.

6. Ask an adult to help you cut the dough into 3- by 12-inch pieces. To assemble twisted bowels, lay one hot dog lengthwise on one 12-inch side of dough and carefully wrap the dough around the hot dog. Press the seam together with your fingers. Slowly bend and curl the bowel into an intestinal shape, then place it on your greased and floured baking sheet. Repeat with the two remaining dough pieces and hot dogs, making each bowel look different.

Note: If you need additional dough to cover bowels, this recipe can be doubled.

7. Repeat steps 5 and 6 with the remaining ball of dough and hot dogs. Use pot holders and, with an adult to help you, place the baking sheet into the oven for 10 to 15 minutes or until bowels turn golden and the hot dogs are warmed through. Have an adult help you remove bowels from oven and allow them to cool slightly before serving. Bowels can also be made a few hours in advance and then served at room temperature.

Makes: 6 bundles of bowels

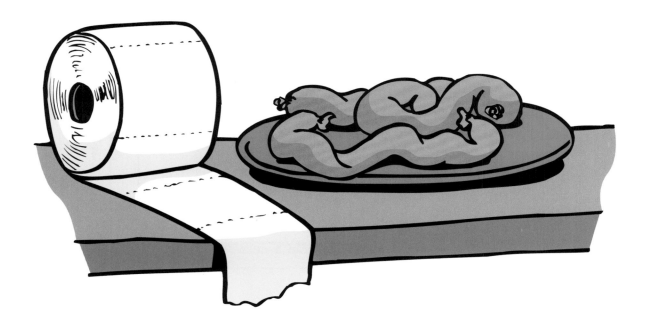

Putrid Presentation
Break a plain chocolate bar into individual squares and rewrap them in aluminum foil. Put these "laxatives" at each person's place setting so their yummy bowel bundles can get on the move after dinner!

Brain Cell Salad

Anyone can mastermind this simple salad!

INGREDIENTS

4 eggs
ice cubes
1 medium onion
4 stalks celery
16-ounce package large elbow macaroni
1 cup mayonnaise
$\frac{1}{4}$ cup sweet pickle relish
1 tablespoon white-wine vinegar
1 tablespoon mustard
$\frac{3}{4}$ teaspoon salt
$\frac{1}{4}$ teaspoon celery seed
black food coloring

Stove Top
TOOLS YOU'LL NEED

- small saucepan
- pot holders
- utility knife
- grater
- large, heavy saucepan
- colander
- large mixing bowl
- small mixing bowl
- rubber spatula
- large, round serving platter

1. With an adult's help, fill a small saucepan with water and bring it to a boil over high heat. Carefully drop the eggs whole, and cook them for 10 minutes. Using pot holders to hold the pan's handle, drain the water without tipping out the eggs. Quickly refill the pan with cold water and ice cubes. Set eggs aside for about 10 minutes to cool completely.

2. Ask an adult to help you use a utility knife to finely chop the onion and celery. Set them aside. When the eggs have completely cooled, crack and peel them. Use a grater to finely shred the eggs. Set them aside.

3. Fill a large, heavy saucepan with water and, with an adult's help, bring it to a boil over high heat. Add the macaroni and cook according to package directions.

4. Place a colander in the sink. With an adult's help, pour out macaroni to drain. Rinse under cold water for two minutes. When macaroni has drained completely, transfer it to a large mixing bowl.

5. In a small mixing bowl, combine the mayonnaise, pickle relish, vinegar, mustard, salt, and celery seed. Use a rubber spatula to blend ingredients thoroughly. Add the food coloring a few drops at a time and stir well. When the mixture turns medium gray, add it to the large mixing bowl. Stir in the onions, celery, and eggs, and gently toss until macaroni is evenly coated.

6. To mold your brain, carefully spoon macaroni mixture onto your serving platter. Use your clean, dry hands to press the mixture into a large, oval brain. Serve immediately or cover tightly with plastic wrap and refrigerate up to three days in advance.

Serves: 12 gray-matter gobblers

Handwiches

A truly handsome finger food you can put together in a snap!

INGREDIENTS

24 slices white or wheat bread
12 slices salami
12 slices American cheese
12 slices turkey
12 slices cheddar cheese
green and black food coloring
1 small carrot, grated
½ cup mayonnaise
12 slices black olive
chopped pimientos, drained (about 1 tablespoon)
squeeze-top bottle of mustard

TOOLS YOU'LL NEED

- pencil
- tracing paper
- scissors
- small serrated knife
- mixing spoon
- small bowl
- small rubber spatula
- large serving patter or individual plates

1. To start, you'll need two hand patterns—left and right hands—big enough to fit on your bread slices without touching the crusts. Use your pencil and tracing paper to sketch them out. Try making fingers slightly crooked at the knuckles, like craggy old hands. Once you're happy with the patterns, cut them out with scissors.

2. Lay one pattern over a slice of bread and, with an adult's help, carefully cut all around the pattern with a small serrated knife. Repeat with 11 more slices. Use the second pattern in the same manner with the remaining 12 slices of bread. Set them aside in two separate piles. Cut all salami and American cheese slices in the same manner with the right-handed pattern and all turkey and cheddar cheese slices with the left-handed pattern. Set them aside in separate piles.

3. With a mixing spoon and small bowl, stir two drops of green food coloring and one drop black food coloring into the mayonnaise and blend well. Mayonnaise should be a light, gangrenous gray-green. If color appears to dark, lighten it with additional mayonnaise.

4. To assemble scarred and jeweled right hands, make an assembly line in this order: right-hand bread slices, gangrenous mayonnaise, American cheese and salami slices, grated carrot, olives, pimientos, and mustard. Use the spatula to carefully spread each slice with mayonnaise. Layer with cheese, then salami on top. Line two or three carrot pieces lengthwise and about four pieces widthwise as stitches on the center of each hand. To add jewelry, push a piece of pimiento into the hole in each olive slice, then place the olive on top of each ring finger. Squirt a small dot of mustard on each fingertip as a fungal nail.

5. To assemble scab-covered left hands, make an assembly line in this order: left-handed bread slices, gangrenous mayonnaise, cheddar cheese and turkey slices, pimientos, and mustard. Use the spatula to spread each slice with mayonnaise. Layer with cheese, then turkey on top. Add several pimientos as scabs, then squirt a small dot of mustard on each fingertip. Add a few dots of gangrenous mayonnaise over some of the scabs to create blobs of pus. Arrange all open-faced sandwiches on the serving patter or individual plates. Serve immediately or cover tightly in plastic wrap and store in the refrigerator up to one day in advance.

Serves: 12 friends who'll lend a hand—one pair per pal

Dynamite Sticks

Guests will blow their tops over this explosively tasty side dish!

INGREDIENTS

3 medium-sized bananas (straighter ones work best)
$\frac{1}{2}$ lemon
3 cups water, divided
6-ounce package red gelatin
6 red, orange, or yellow gumdrops
6 chow mein noodles

Stove Top

TOOLS YOU'LL NEED

- paring knife
- 2 medium mixing bowls
- medium saucepan
- pot holders
- large spoon
- 6 empty 6-ounce frozen juice concentrate cardboard cans
- serving plates
- can opener (not electric)

1. With an adult's help, peel the bananas and slice them in half widthwise with a paring knife. Place them into a mixing bowl and squeeze juice from the lemon over the bananas to prevent them from turning brown. Set aside.

2. With an adult's help, bring 2 cups water (plus a bit extra to allow for evaporation) to a boil in a saucepan. Using pot holders, pour 2 cups boiling water into a second mixing bowl. Pour in gelatin and stir well with a large spoon to dissolve gelatin completely. Pour in 1 cup very cold water and stir. Place the mixing bowl in the refrigerator for about 15 minutes to thicken slightly.

3. To assemble the dynamic sticks, place a spoonful of slightly thickened gelatin into each empty 6-ounce can, the firecracker mold. Insert one banana half into each can with the flat, cut portion down. Center each banana in the can so that it does not hit the sides. Also, the banana should not extend beyond the can's rim, so trim off any excess. Spoon the remaining gelatin evenly into the cans. Place the cans in the refrigerator for about three hours or until gelatin is firm.

4. Meanwhile, to create flaming dynamite wicks, wedge one gumdrop onto each chow mein noodle. Set aside.

5. When the dynamite sticks are firm, take them out of the refrigerator. Dip each can up to the rim in warm water for about 30 seconds. Do not allow the water to touch the gelatin dynamite stick. Then invert each can onto individual serving plates. With an adult's help, use a can opener to poke a small hole into the bottom of the juice can. The dynamite sticks will easily slide out onto the plates. You can make your dynamite sticks up to one week in advance and store, tightly covered, in plastic wrap in the refrigerator. Do not remove dynamite sticks from their molds until you're ready to serve.

6. Insert one gumdrop wick into each dynamite stick and serve.

Serves: 6 explosive personalities

Putrid Presentation

Tape several inflated balloons underneath the table where guests will be eating and hide a large safety pin nearby. As guests cut into their dynamite, slide your hand under the table and explode a balloon!

Bad Breath Biscuits

Here's a smelly dish fit for all your bad breath buddies!

INGREDIENTS

12-ounce jar fire-roasted red bell peppers, packed in oil
6 slices bologna
$\frac{1}{4}$ cup butter
$\frac{3}{4}$ cup cornmeal
$\frac{3}{4}$ cup flour
2 teaspoons baking powder
$\frac{1}{2}$ teaspoon salt
1 egg
$\frac{2}{3}$ cup milk
$\frac{1}{4}$ cup sugar
$1\frac{1}{2}$ cups fresh frozen whole-kernel corn, thawed on paper towels, divided

Oven and Microwave/Stove Top

TOOLS YOU'LL NEED

- cutting board
- paring knife
- pot holders
- large mixing bowl
- whisk
- small mixing bowl
- small ladle
- 12-capacity muffin tray, well greased
- wire rack

1. Open and drain the peppers and lay them on a cutting board. With an adult's help, use your paring knife to carve out 12 pairs of lips. Make each one wide enough to cover the top of a muffin without hanging over. Set them aside.

2. To prepare coated tongues, cut bologna circles in half-moon shapes using a paring knife. (Always ask an adult to help you when using a knife.) Next, cut the sides off of each slice to create a natural-looking tongue shape with a rounded tip. Set aside.

3. Ask an adult to help you preheat the oven to 400 degrees. Place butter into a microwave-safe liquid-measuring cup. Place it in the microwave on high (100%) for about 20 seconds or until completely melted. (Butter may also be melted in a small saucepan on your stove top.) With an adult's help, use pot holders to remove the butter from the microwave and set aside.

4. Pour the cornmeal, flour, baking powder, and salt into a large mixing bowl. Gently stir using a whisk. Crack the egg in a small mixing bowl and whisk together with the milk and sugar until thoroughly combined. Pour the egg mixture into the cornmeal mixture. Stir in the melted butter and 1 cup thawed, drained corn. (Reserve the rest for making rotten teeth.)

5. With a small ladle, divide the biscuit batter into the well-greased muffin cups. Then lay one pair of lips over the top of each biscuit, parted enough to fit in a row of rotten corn teeth and a tongue as shown.

6. With an adult's help, place the biscuits in the oven and bake for 15 to 18 minutes or until biscuits turn golden. With pot holders, carefully remove biscuits from oven and place the tray on a wire rack to cool slightly before serving. Bad Breath Biscuits can be made up to two weeks in advance and stored, frozen, in a tightly sealed container. (Lay biscuits flat—do not stack them in the freezer.) A few hours before serving, place them in the refrigerator to thaw. To warm biscuits before serving, arrange them on a foil-lined baking sheet. Cover them lightly with a second layer of foil, and heat at 350 degrees for about 10 minutes or until warmed through.

Serves: 12 odor eaters

Beastly Beverages

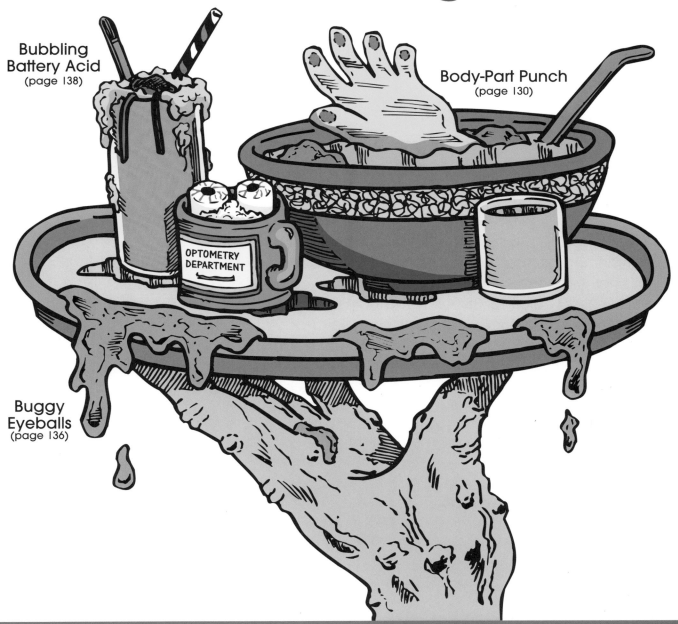

Bubbling
Battery Acid
(page 138)

Body-Part Punch
(page 130)

Buggy
Eyeballs
(page 136)

OPTOMETRY
DEPARTMENT

Read, Sing, and Play Along! Gross and Annoying Songs   **129**

Body-Part Punch

Give yourself a hand—this punch looks like hard work, but it's not. And your friends are sure to give you a standing ovation.

INGREDIENTS

red and yellow food coloring
5 red gumdrops
½ gallon lime sherbet, softened
1 large package lime-flavored presweetened, powdered drink mix
2 liters lemon-lime soda, well chilled

TOOLS YOU'LL NEED

- new rubber glove
- pitcher
- long-handled spoon
- rubber band
- ice-cream scooper
- large punch bowl
- ladle
- cups

1. You'll need to prepare your floating body part at least one day in advance. First, thoroughly rinse out your rubber glove. Fill your pitcher with water. Add one drop red food coloring and one drop yellow food coloring. Stir with long-handled spoon. The color should be light peach. (For darker skin tones use chocolate milk rather than colored water.) Wedge one gumdrop into each fingertip of the glove. Then have someone hold the glove open while you pour the colored water into the glove. Leave enough room to secure the end tightly with a rubber band. Place the glove in the freezer overnight. For ease in unmolding, be sure the fingers lay straight while freezing.

2. Clear enough space in your refrigerator to fit the punch bowl. About one hour before you're ready to serve the punch, scoop the softened sherbet into the punch bowl and add the powdered drink mix. Stir together using the long-handled spoon and refrigerate.

3. Just before serving, remove the glove from the freezer. Peel the glove off the hand. You may need to run it under warm water to help loosen the glove. Take the sherbet mixture out of the refrigerator and put the frozen hand in it. Add the chilled lemon-lime soda, stir well, and serve.

Serves: About 12 body slammers

Putrid Presentation
To make each glass especially disgusting, serve with a few Toenail Trimmings (see page 92).

Pesticide Punch

This punch may paralyze any insect pests, but it will leave your bug-crazed buddies buzzing for more!

INGREDIENTS

12 gummi fish
6 black mini jelly beans
6 gummi worms
6 fizzing drink tablets, any flavor
1 quart lemon-lime soda, well chilled
1 quart blue-colored sports drink, well chilled
1 cup chocolate jimmie sprinkles

TOOLS YOU'LL NEED

- 2 ice cube trays
- large reclosable plastic bags
- rolling pin
- large pitcher
- long-handled spoon
- tall glasses
- iced-tea spoons

1. You'll need to prepare your dead fish and bugs the day before you plan to serve them. Place one gummi fish, headfirst, in each of the 12 openings in one ice cube tray. It's okay if the tails hang outside the tray. Fill the other tray with six black jelly beans on one side and six gummi worms on the other. Let the worms' excess length hang over the sides. Slowly fill each tray with water and freeze overnight.

2. Place the fizzing drink tablets into a large reclosable bag. Remove excess air and seal the bag. To crush the tablets into pesticide powder, firmly roll the rolling pin back and forth over the bag until the tablets are finely ground. Set aside.

3. In a large pitcher, mix together the lemon-lime soda and sports drink with a long-handled spoon.

4. To assemble, place about 2 tablespoons jimmie sprinkles into the bottom of each glass as a sandy layer. Empty the ice cube trays and fill each glass with a dead fish, a bug, a second dead fish, and top with a worm. Be sure the worm dangles over the glass's rim.

5. Slowly fill each glass with the blue soda mixture. Just before serving this toxic treat, stir in a teaspoon of pesticide powder using individual iced-tea spoons and watch it fizz! If you'd like to get a head start on this deadly drink, you can do steps 1 and 2 two to three weeks in advance. Then, on the day of your party, follow steps 3 through 5.

Serves: 6 party bugs

Bowl o' Bile

Don't lose your lunch—save it! A bowl brimming with projectile punch adds a gutsy flair to any gastronomic get-together!

INGREDIENTS

3 cups water, divided
3 medium-sized ripe bananas, peeled
1 cup sugar
12-ounce can frozen orange juice concentrate, thawed
$\frac{3}{4}$ cup frozen lemonade concentrate, thawed
3 cups unsweetened pineapple juice
3 liters lemon-lime soda, well chilled
1 cup mini marshmallows

TOOLS YOU'LL NEED

- large punch bowl (one that can be frozen)
- blender
- long-handled spoon
- plastic wrap
- potato masher
- ladle
- cups

1. Clear enough room in your freezer to fit the punch bowl. Place the punch bowl on your work surface.

2. Place 1 cup water, the bananas, and the sugar into a blender. With an adult's help, blend on medium speed until bananas are smooth but slightly chunky, about 15 to 20 seconds.

3. Pour banana mixture into punch bowl and add orange juice concentrate, lemonade concentrate, pineapple juice, and remaining 2 cups water. Stir well with long-handled spoon. Wrap the bowl tightly in plastic wrap and freeze two to three hours or overnight. You can freeze the bile mixture up to one week in advance of your party.

4. Remove your bowl of bile from the freezer about two hours before guests arrive. Just before serving, mash bile to a chunky consistency using potato masher. Note: If your punch bowl is made of glass, use extra caution and have an adult hold the bowl steady while you break up the bile. Pour in the chilled soda and mini marshmallows (bile chunks), stir, and serve.

Serves: About 24 stomach pumpers

Putrid Presentation

Peel the label off an empty bottle of liquid antacid and attach it to a clean glass bottle. Fill it with whole milk and color it pink using red food coloring. As guests are sipping your retched-up refreshment, offer them a spoonful of your stomach-soothing medication.

Read, Sing, and Play Along! Gross and Annoying Songs

Buggy Eyeballs

Bugged-out, bulging eyeballs are the eye-deal adornment for this oozing warm beverage.

INGREDIENTS

16 large marshmallows
16 black jelly beans
red food coloring
$\frac{1}{2}$ gallon milk
8 1-ounce envelopes hot cocoa mix
$\frac{1}{2}$ cup creamy peanut butter
1 can whipped topping

Stove Top

TOOLS YOU'LL NEED

- kitchen scissors
- 16 red-and-white striped straws
- small saucer
- toothpick
- large saucepan
- wooden spoon
- 8 mugs

1. With the scissors, trim each straw so that it extends about 2 inches beyond the rim of a mug. Snip an X into the tall side portion of each marshmallow, cutting about halfway into each. Wedge one jelly bean into the opening. Gently squeeze the marshmallow around the jelly bean to form a beady black eye. Repeat with the remaining marshmallows.

2. Carefully wedge one straw into the bottom of each marshmallow eyeball a little more than halfway in. Squirt several drops of red food coloring into a small saucer.

3. Dip the tip of a toothpick into the food coloring, then drag it randomly over the marshmallow to create veins. Repeat this several times, crossing over the veins so that the eyes appear bloodshot. Repeat with the remaining marshmallow eyeballs. (You can prepare Buggy Eyeballs up to two days in advance and store them, loosely covered, at room temperature until you're ready to garnish your beverage.)

4. Just before serving, pour the milk into a large saucepan. With an adult's help, heat the milk over medium heat, stirring constantly with a wooden spoon. When the milk is very warm but not boiling, stir in the packets of cocoa mix and peanut butter. Continue stirring over low heat until all ingredients are thoroughly mixed.

5. Line up the mugs on your work surface. Ask an adult to help you evenly pour the cocoa mixture into the mugs. Place two Buggy Eyeballs in each mug and top with a squirt of whipped topping. Serve immediately.

Serves: 8 peeper poppers

Putrid Presentation
Add an elegant flair for all the female eyeball eaters on your guest list! Insert eyelashes (tiny snips of black shoelace licorice) into the top of each pair of girl's eyeballs.

Bubbling Battery Acid

Look what someone dragged in from the garage—an old, corroded battery, just oozing its juices. Drink up!

INGREDIENTS

1 quart chocolate ice cream
$\frac{1}{2}$ cup strawberry-flavored syrup
1 quart milk
yellow food coloring
1 quart seltzer water, well chilled
8 ropes each red and black licorice

TOOLS YOU'LL NEED

- 8 tall glasses
- ice-cream scooper
- iced-tea spoons
- blender

1. Evenly divide the ice cream into the tall glasses with the ice-cream scooper. Place one iced-tea spoon into each glass.

2. Pour the syrup and milk into a blender. Then, with an adult's help, blend on medium speed for about five seconds. Add four or five drops of yellow food coloring per serving and the chilled seltzer, and blend again for five seconds.

3. Quickly pour the seltzer mixture into the glasses and serve while the battery acid is still bubbling and foaming. Dangle a rope of red licorice for the positive charge and a rope of black licorice for the negative charge over each glass.

Serves: 8 maniac mechanics

Crafts, Games, Skits, and Jokes

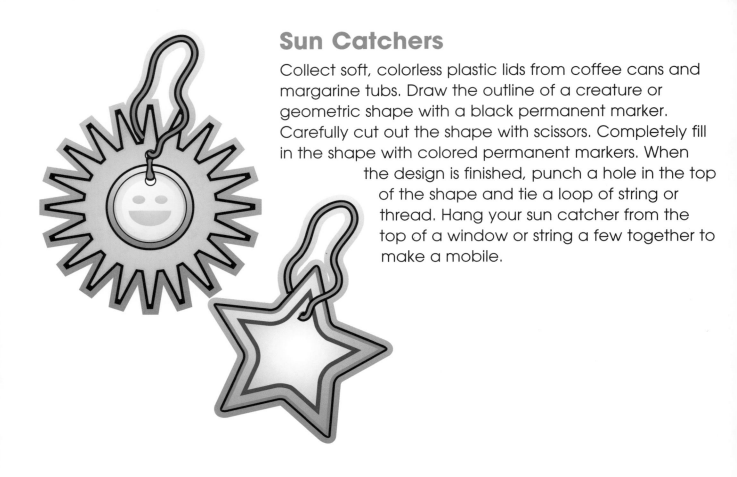

Sun Catchers

Collect soft, colorless plastic lids from coffee cans and margarine tubs. Draw the outline of a creature or geometric shape with a black permanent marker. Carefully cut out the shape with scissors. Completely fill in the shape with colored permanent markers. When the design is finished, punch a hole in the top of the shape and tie a loop of string or thread. Hang your sun catcher from the top of a window or string a few together to make a mobile.

 ## Snow Sculptures

Mix up some wintertime fun no matter what time of year it is or where you live! In a large bowl mix 2 cups of mild, powdered laundry detergent, add water, and whip with an electric mixer until doughy. Mold and sculpt the snow mixture. When you're finished, allow the sculpture to dry. The snow will dry bright white.

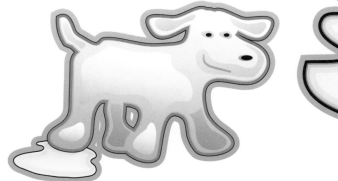

Blue Goop

All kids love goop—called by any number of gross and disgusting names! Follow this recipe to make your own goop.

You'll need:
- White glue
- Water
- 2 paper cups
- Blue food coloring
- Borax laundry detergent (available from a grocery store)
- Small plastic storage container

Mix together 2 tablespoons of white glue and 2 tablespoons of water in a paper cup. In another paper cup, mix together ten drops of blue food coloring, $\frac{1}{4}$ cup of water, and $\frac{3}{4}$ teaspoon of borax laundry detergent. Add 2 tablespoons of the borax mixture to the glue mixture and stir well. Have fun playing with your Blue Goop. Store it in an airtight container.

To avoid stains, be careful not to let Blue Goop touch furniture, carpet, or clothing.

Rubberband Ball

To make your own bouncy ball, pinch together the ends of a single rubber band and tie it into a loose double knot. Wrap and twist a second band around the knot repeatedly, until it is taut. Continue adding rubber bands one at a time until the ball is as large as you like, or you run out of bands. You also can speed along the process by covering an inner core of wadded-up newspaper or aluminum foil with rubber bands.

Our Town

Name yourself as the mayor of this homemade city!

You'll need:
- Brown or white paper lunch bags
- Newspapers
- Markers, crayons, paint
- Construction paper, fabric scraps and other art materials

Build an entire city of brown paper lunch bags. Use two bags for each building. On one bag draw or color a building—either horizontally or vertically. Add bricks or siding, sketch in doors and windows, window boxes, stairwells, signs, and even people! Next, stuff the second bag with crumpled newspaper and slip the decorated bag on top. Cut out signs, awnings, chimneys, overhanging rooftops, and doors from colored paper, and glue them onto the buildings. Set up the city on the floor or on a table.

Alien Invasion

Okay, so they haven't really come from outer space to take over the world. These one-of-a-kind aliens are still fun to make!

You'll need:
- Balloons
- Cardboard, poster board
- Markers
- Scissors

To make each alien, first make its feet or base: cut out a heart or butterfly shape from poster board or cardboard. Draw on shoes or toes with markers, crayons, or paint. When done, cut a 1/2-inch slit between the heels. Blow up a balloon for each pair of feet and knot the end. Using markers, carefully draw the alien's face and body directly on the balloon. Slip the knotted end of the balloon into the slit between the feet. Stand your alien balloons around the room, or place them where unsuspecting friends will find them.

Gumdrop Construction Project

Empty a bag of gumdrops, set out a package of toothpicks, and start to build! Begin making and combining triangles and squares. Experiment and discover what formations are sturdier and stronger. The candies will dry out and crumble—so don't plan on saving the creations! Here's another great idea—demolish the project with a Gumdrop Eating Contest!

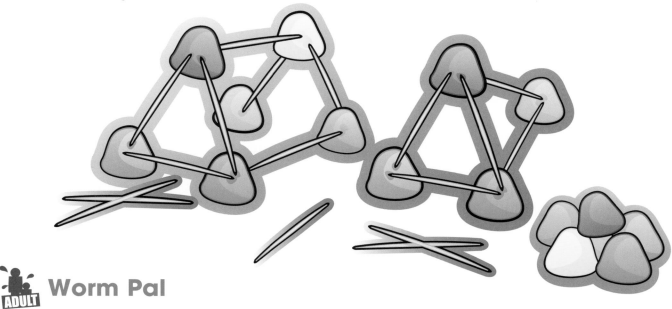

Worm Pal

You and your friends can make and care for your own pet worms! For more fun, make an extra long snake!

You'll need:
- Fabric scraps
- Sewing machine or needle and thread
- Stuffing material (available at a craft or discount store)
- Craft wire or thin wire coat hanger, cut as long as your worm
- Pins
- Scissors

Measure and cut a 3-inch by 12-inch rectangle from scrap fabric—fleece material works well. Fold the fabric in half lengthwise, right side together (inside out), and pin. Carefully round the corners with the scissors—after all no one has ever seen a square-ended worm! Now, carefully sew along the edges, leaving one end open. Turn the worm right side out. Insert craft wire or even a wire coat hanger cut to the length of your worm. Fill the worm with stuffing, keeping the wire in the center. When the worm is stuffed full, sew the end together. Bend and shape your new pet worm. Add eyes, a tongue, stripes, dots, and other markings with paint or glued-on fabric scraps.

Gruesome Monster Heads

These shrunken apple heads may take some time, but they're guaranteed to be a scream!

You'll need:
- Peeled apples
- Small paring knife
- Supplies for making hair and facial features— yarn, beads, feathers, dried beans, rice, pasta, toothpicks
- Craft sticks
- Cups or mugs

With adult supervision, carefully carve eyes, nose, and a mouth into each peeled apple. Don't worry if the carvings aren't perfect—this will make the head look even creepier. Poke rice, beans, dried corn, raisins, or pasta into the apple to make facial features and hair. Be creative! When finished, push a craft stick into the bottom of each apple, and prop upright in a cup or mug in a warm, dry place. Make sure the apple is not touching the side of the cup. Visit the monsters-in-progress every few days. When the apple heads begin to turn leathery you can change facial expressions by gently twisting, pushing, pulling, turning, and rearranging items. In a few weeks you'll have really gruesome monster heads.

Cracker Castle

Forget the gingerbread cookies! Build a haunted castle with assorted crackers and peanut butter instead!

You'll need:
- Assorted crackers
- Peanut butter
- Raisins, nuts, candy pieces, etc.
- Cookie sheet or wax paper

Build your castle on a cookie sheet or large piece of waxed paper. Use plain soda crackers, large and bite-sized butter crackers, club crackers, square wheat crackers, graham crackers, round vanilla wafers, and sandwich cookies. Set crackers vertically, gluing them to each other with peanut butter. You might want to spread a peanut butter foundation and set the crackers into it. Glue smaller crackers onto larger ones to make doors, window shutters, columns, and stairs. Use plain or cinnamon graham crackers for sloped roofs. Add raisins, cereal, pasta, seeds, or anything else that can be attached with peanut butter.

Spider Web T-shirts

You'll need:
- An old white T-shirt
- Black dye
- An old bucket
- Rubber bands
- Permanent markers or fabric paint

What to do:

1. Fill a bucket with black dye following the package directions.
2. Lay an old white T-shirt flat on the table. Pull the T-shirt up from the center and put rubber bands around the "wad" of material. Continue pulling up from the center and adding more rubber bands. The more rubber bands you use, the more your shirt will look like a spider's web.
3. Submerge the whole T-shirt in the bucket of black dye. Follow the package directions. The longer you leave the shirt in the dye, the darker your spider's web will become.
4. Remove the t-shirt from the dye, carefully wring out the excess water, and lay the shirt flat on the floor or table. Allow the shirt to dry completely before removing the rubber bands.
5. Use a permanent marker or fabric paint to draw your spider in its web.

Foil Mask

You'll need:
- Heavy-duty aluminum foil
- Scissors
- Permanent markers

Cut a 24- by-12-inch piece of heavy-duty aluminum foil. Fold the foil into a 12-inch square. Working together with a friend, press the foil onto your friend's face, making sure to mold it over his or her cheekbones, nose, lips, and eye sockets. Carefully pull the mask away. Now, have your friend mold your face mask. Use scissors to cut eye, nose, and mouth holes. Add colorful details with a permanent marker, pressing down gently.

Gross Eating Contest

Ahead of time, fill two paper grocery bags with food items that smell or feel gross—nothing spoiled! Each bag must have the same items. Suggestions: raw onions, cold beans, cooked spaghetti, hardboiled eggs, black olives, cheese chunks, and lunchmeat. Divide your friends or family members into two teams. The first player on each team takes one item from the bag, eats it completely, and then passes the bag to the next player. The first team to eat all the food items in the bag is the winner!

Belching Contest

Players try burping as many letters in the alphabet as they can. Whoever makes it the furthest through the alphabet wins! Give prizes for the loudest burps, softest burps, most disgusting burps… ooooo, yuck!

Soda Roulette

You'll need a can of soda for each player. Gather outside. Vigorously shake one can of soda. Mix the cans up. Each player chooses a can, puts it up to his nose, and on the count of three opens it! Who is the unlucky winner?

Mind Reader

One of your friends must think of a person, place, or thing! You must read his or her mind! You can only ask questions that he or she can answer by saying "yes" or "no." How many questions will you have to ask? Now, it's your turn to think of a person, place, or thing and your friend's turn to ask questions.

Alphabetical Tall Tale

Choose a subject—any subject! Maybe the subject is scary movies, or disgusting foods, or an alien invasion from outer space, or a mad scientist and an experiment that's gone wrong—any subject that will make a great story. Now, begin the story. The first player says a sentence beginning with the letter "A." The second player adds more to the story, beginning a sentence with the letter "B." Try to get as far down the alphabet as you can. It's harder than it sounds!

Example: *"Aliens have invaded!"*
          "Bravo! "
          "Cool kids are trying to capture the aliens."
          "Demented doctors are attempting to destroy the aliens!"

For more challenging fun, try to tell the story asking only questions! Every player must ask a question that begins with the letter of the alphabet.

Candy Throw-Up

Most of your friends know what it feels like to have eaten too much candy! But do they know what their favorite candies look like when it's…let's say, come back up? Ahead of time, ask an adult to help you melt 6-10 candy bars in individual cupcake or muffin liners in a microwave. (Be certain to write down what candy bar you melted in each container!) Players pass and smell each container of candy throw-up and write down what name brand candy product they believe was "regurgitated."

For even more disgusting fun, put the melted candies in disposable diapers. Your friends must smell each diaper and guess what candy the baby passed!

Pig

You and a small group of friends will quickly pass the time with this classic game of strategy and chance.

You'll need:
- A die
- Paper
- Pencil

Take turns rolling a die and adding up your points. You can roll as many times as you want, but if you roll a 1, you lose all your points for that turn. When you choose to stop, write your score and pass the die to the next player. The first player to reach 100 points wins.

Flashlight Signals

Play this game outside after dark with a large group of friends under adult supervision. Every player will need a flashlight! To begin, pair off with another friend, and create your own unique flashlight signal—for example, one short and one long flash followed by three short flashes. The partners separate and go to opposite ends of a large playing area. Each pair tries to reunite as quickly as possible by sending flashlight signals to each other. The first pair to reunite is the winner.

Pop Up Minute

Okay, just how long do you think a minute really is? What about two minutes, five minutes? Try this with a group of friends. Out of sight of any clocks or watches, ask your friends to stand up when they feel one minute is up! Use one watch to time your friends. The friend who stands up closest to the minute is the winner. For more fun, try two minutes, three minutes, or even five minutes.

Beat the Bunny

The object of the game is for the farmer to catch the bunny. No, we're not talking about a real farmer trapping a real bunny! This is a really fast game to play with a group of friends. You'll need two balls of different sizes. Players sit on the floor in a circle. Begin passing the bunny—the small ball—from player to player around the circle. When the bunny is about half way around, start passing the farmer—the large ball—in the same direction. Can players pass the farmer fast enough to catch up with the bunny? For more challenging play, the farmer can change directions, but the bunny can only go one way.

Odds/Evens

Play this game with another friend when you have a few minutes to spare. (This is great fun while waiting for your food at a sit-down restaurant—just don't get too loud!) One of you chooses to be "odds" and the other chooses to be "evens." Both of you make a fist, shake it, say, "One, two, three...shoot," and stick out one or two fingers. Count the fingers that are sticking out. If the total is an odd number, the player who picked odds wins that number of points; and the same goes for evens. The first player to reach 50 points wins.

Ghost

Next time you have several friends together, try this challenging spelling and bluffing game. To start, one friend says a letter of the alphabet. Each friend adds a letter but is careful not to spell a word. If a player does make a word he's the ghost and is out of the game. On your turn, try to say a letter that forces the next player to make a word. But be careful, because the next player may challenge you and ask what word you're spelling! If you can't give a word you lose the challenge and are out of the game. But if you do have a word in mind, the challenger loses and is out of the game. For even more fun, players who complete a word or lose a challenge must do a stunt acceptable to the group.

Fast Talker

Now you can prove who in your group of friends talks too much! Challenge each friend to talk non-stop for one minute about a subject you choose. It's harder than you think! If the player hesitates or stops talking he is out of the game. You'll need someone with a watch or stopwatch to time each player. For more challenging play, have two friends talk at the same time about that topic for one minute.

Where's "It"?

Play this twisted game of Hide and Seek outside after dark under adult supervision! "It" hides while all the other kids count to 50. Everyone looks for "It," but when they find him each quietly hides with "It." Soon, those who are left realize that they alone are looking for "It."

Blanket Stand

Spread out a blanket on the floor. The object of the game is to have your entire group of friends on the blanket so that no arms, legs, or other body parts are touching the ground off the blanket. If this is too easy, have your friends get off the blanket, fold the blanket in half, and try again. Keep folding the blanket in half! Soon, you'll end up in a big pile! Guaranteed!

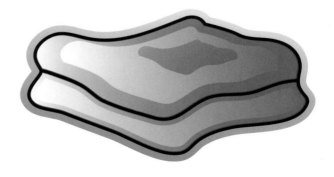

Worms in a Pie

You'll need gummi worms, whipped cream, and aluminum pie plates or deep disposable plates—one for each person playing the game. Place the same amount of gummi worms on each plate and cover them with whipped cream. Blindfold each player. On the count of three, each player dips into the pie with their mouth, trying to pull out as many worms as they can. See who can pull out the most worms in a time limit or just set a certain amount of worms to find. For more fun, and if everyone is willing, put all the gummi worms and whipped cream in one large container and let players search together.

Putt, Putt Golf

Miniature golfing every day may be out of the question! But here is a fun, inexpensive way to practice your game at home or at a restaurant while you wait for your food to arrive!

You'll need:
- Plain paper
- Markers, crayons
- Blindfolds—if you don't trust players to close their eyes!

Use a large sheet of copy paper or construction paper. Draw the fairway—an odd, oblong shape. At one end draw a line for the tee (or starting point). At the far end of the fairway draw a small circle—this is the hole! Now, place a marker, crayon, or pencil down at the tee, close your eyes, and try to draw a line to the hole! Open your eyes and lift the marker; that's your shot. Add a stroke if you strayed outside the boundaries. The next player then tees off on the same sheet. Play again, beginning where your last stroke ended. Your score is the number of shots it takes you to reach the hole. Play nine holes or even 18 like the pros.

"Sticky Fingers"

Choose one friend to be "Sticky Fingers." In this game of tag, when "Sticky Fingers" tags you, place your hand on the place he touched and continue to run. As more and more friends become stuck on themselves, "Sticky Fingers" has a better chance to totally immobilize someone. A third touch and you're out of the game.

Snake in the Grass

Mark off a small playing area outside. One friend is the snake, and lies on the ground on his stomach. Everyone gathers fearlessly around him. When you shout, "Snake in the grass" everyone moves, staying within the playing area. The snake, moving on his belly, tries to tag as many as he can. If you're tagged, you become a snake, too. The last person caught is the snake starter in the next game. Make the playing area fairly small.

Ankle Wrestling

First, mark off a small playing area. Next, choose two friends to enter the ring, stoop over, and grasp their ankles. The object of the game is to push your opponent over or to make him let go of his ankles. The player is automatically disqualified if he steps out of the ring. Set up a tournament with friends and family and declare an Ankle Wrestling Champ.

Sock Wrestling

Mark off a small play area. Players take off their shoes, but leave on their socks and move around the ring. The idea of the game is for players to somehow remove a sock from their opponents. It can be played one-on-one or with several players in the ring at the same time. Players who lose both socks must leave the ring.

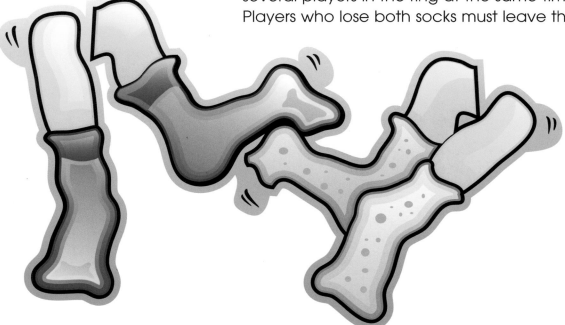

Teeny-Tiny Scavenger Hunt

Send your friends outside in search of as many different natural items as they can find that fit in a small, plastic condiment container. Consider awarding points for each unique item collected, and extra points for live creatures that will be returned to nature, of course! If you go to a park be certain you have permission to disturb or remove natural items from the grounds.

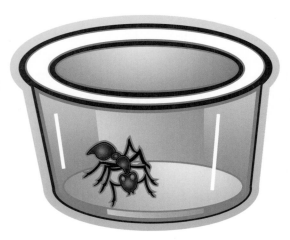

Nauseating Nature Hunt

If the Teeny-Tiny Scavenger Hunt is too tame for your tastes, search instead for icky, nasty natural items.

Make a list of icky items and the points that will be earned for each item that is found. Take a grocery bag and go out into the yard to find the items. Whoever gets the most points, wins.

Icky Items May Include:
- A dead moth
- Spoonful of tree sap
- Daddy long-legs
- Green caterpillar guts
- Squished berries
- A four-leaf clover
- A live slug
- A live worm
- Ants
- Moss
- Stinkweed
- A dead fly
- Snake
- Cricket

Spud

Gather your friends together, everyone touching home base, and have each player count off. One player who is "It" throws a ball high in the air and calls out one player's number. As the other players scatter, the called player catches the ball and shouts, "Spud!" The other players must immediately freeze. The ball holder takes two giant steps toward any player, and tries to hit that player with the ball. The target person can try to dodge the ball by moving his body but not his feet. If the thrower misses OR the target catches the ball, the thrower earns an S. If he hits the target, that person earns an S. Whoever earns the letter becomes the next "It" and begins the next round. Players are eliminated once they earn S-P-U-D.

Knots

Stand your friends in a circle facing each other, shake hands with the person directly across from you, and join left hands with a different person in the group. Now, try to untangle the human knot without letting go of your hands. Try doing this with different size groups.

Magic Number

The object of the game is to force a player to say the magic number. To play, first choose a magic number—almost any number that you can count to quickly! On your turn, say only one OR two numbers next in the sequence. For example, say the magic number is 20. Player one counts "One, Two." The next player may say, "Three, Four." The next player may say, "Five." Play continues until a player is forced to say 20, the Magic Number. That player is out of the game. Continue playing until a champion is named! This game requires concentration and forward thinking!

Fortunately-Unfortunately

Look at the bright side of things in a silly way! For example, you say, "Unfortunately, there's a big brown bear in the car." Your friend says, "Fortunately, he doesn't eat girls." Another friend says, "Unfortunately, he's looking at me and licking his lips." You say, "Fortunately, I brought along my brown-bear-catching sword." Continue alternating between fortunate and unfortunate things until everyone breaks down with laughter.

Grass Blade Symphony

With a blade of grass and a little practice, anyone can make beautiful music! Try this stunt with several friends and soon your unusual musical talents will annoy everyone nearby.

First, find a nice wide blade of grass, about as long as your first finger. Make a loose fist, with your thumb pointing upwards and your thumbnail towards you. Now, lick the edge of your thumb from wrist to tip and stick the blade where you licked. Sure, it's gross, but the moisture keeps the blade of grass from falling off. Then bring your other hand and thumb up so that the grass is trapped between your thumbs. You should see a gap between the first and second joints of your thumb where the grass is not touching either thumb. Be sure that the grass is stretched tightly in this gap. Put your thumbs to your mouth, so that this gap is against your lips. Pucker your lips, as if you were going to blow out a candle, and blow hard. If you do it just right, you will hear a loud sound. Depending on the shape of the blade of grass, how tight it is, and how hard you blow, you may get anything from a low rasp to a loud, shrill whistle. With some practice, you can make a variety of sounds.

Toothpaste and Germs

Divide your friends into two teams, "Toothpaste" and "Germs" respectively. Send team Toothpaste to one side of the playground or yard and team Germs to the other side. The leader gives each side commands in turn. For example, "Germs, advance 3," and then the Germs take 3 steps forward. "Toothpaste, retreat 2," and the Toothpaste go 2 steps backwards. Once you have them reasonably near to each other say, "Toothpaste (or Germs) ATTACK." Then the team you have chosen chases the others back to their safety. Any players tagged then join the other side and the game starts again. Keep it going for as long as you need!

Cloud Watching

If you can't go out after dark and count the stars, head to a hillside or wide-open space, stretch out on a blanket and look up at clouds in the sky! What shapes are they making? Time them to see how fast they float by.

Star Gazing

Spend an hour or two after dark, kicking back on a hillside, looking up at the night sky. Have several binoculars to share—perhaps a telescope —and count the stars, play imaginary dot to dot with the stars or make up stories about the stars. For more serious learning, use constellation guide maps and try to locate the constellations.

Spitball Target Practice

You'll never want to play darts again after using spitballs instead! First, make a target on a piece of poster board, like a dartboard with circles and points marked off. (Of course, with permission, you might draw your dartboard on a sliding glass door using dry-erase or washable markers.) Next, each player must make his arsenal of spitballs. Give each player a different color piece of paper. Each player shreds the paper into small pieces, wets them in his mouth, rolling them into tiny balls with his tongue. Finally, give each player a straw. Aiming ONLY at the target, load one spitball (or two, or three!) and blow them out! Keep score, adding up the points of each spitball that actually sticks! Never blow the spitballs at someone else!

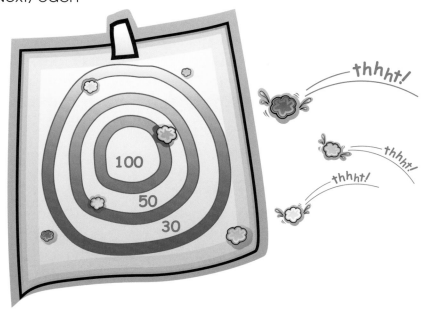

Bobbing For Apples

This classic game is perfect on a hot day! Put several apples in a large tub or wading pool. Players try to grab one using only their mouth. For more fun, add ice cubes to the water.

Try this with younger kids: Cut several apple shapes out of construction paper and place a loop of masking tape on each one. Place the apples in a large clothesbasket, box, or pan. To bob for the apples, a blindfolded player must get an apple by touching his nose to the masking tape!

Face-To-Face

Choose one player to stand in the center, while the rest of you stand in a large circle face-to-face with a partner. The player in the middle calls out commands such as "Face-to-face," "Back-to-back," "Side-to-side," or "Knee-to-Knee." Players take these positions accordingly. When the person in the middle calls "All change!" all the players must find a new partner! The person in the middle tries to find a partner, too. The person left without a partner becomes the new person in the middle and starts to give commands.

Read, Sing, and Play Along! Gross and Annoying Songs **155**

Ice Fishing

Ahead of time fill several large buckets with ice water and marbles. Hide the buckets until time to play. Divide your friends into teams. Everyone removes their shoes and socks. Explain that in this relay race, each team member runs to the bucket, puts his bare foot into the water, pulls out as many marbles as possible on just one try using only toes, places the marbles in a container, and runs back to the team. The next player repeats. Of course, leave out the detail about ice water! The team that pulls the most marbles from the ice water is the winner.

Master and Commander

Have your friends sit in a circle on the floor. Choose one person to leave the room for a few minutes. While that friend is out of the room, choose one person in the group to be the Master and Commander. Everyone in the group repeats the actions of the Master and Commander. If he scratches his nose, everyone slowly begins to scratch their noses, too. If the Master and Commander places his hands behind his head, everyone else slowly places their hands behind their heads. After you've practiced following the Master and Commander, bring the first person back into the room. The object of the game is for that person to guess who is the Master and Commander. When the Master and Commander is revealed, he leaves the room and becomes the next person to guess.

Water Balloon Volleyball

Form several teams. Team members each hold on to the sides of an old bed sheet or large beach towel. Work together to toss a water balloon to the other team. Keep score, if you want, as you would in regular volleyball matches.

Ice Melt

Ahead of time, fill several half-gallon milk containers with water and freeze. Add a toy action figure to each container. To play, give each team one block of ice with the carton removed. The first team to rescue the action figure by melting their block of ice using only their hands is the winner. Consider allowing team members to use their feet and other body parts, too—but this can be, well, a little gross! Another option is to melt the ice by pouring warm water over the ice block.

Wink

One friend leaves the room. The remaining players sit in a circle and select their group leader. The first friend returns to the center of the circle. Now, the group leader secretly winks at another player seated around the circle; that player waits several seconds and then falls or collapses, pretending to gag, fall to the floor in pain, or just faint. The leader continues to secretly wink at other players who each collapse. The object is for the friend in the center to identify the secret leader. At any time the player may point to someone in the circle and say, "I accuse you." When the secret leader is revealed, he leaves the room and becomes the next person to guess.

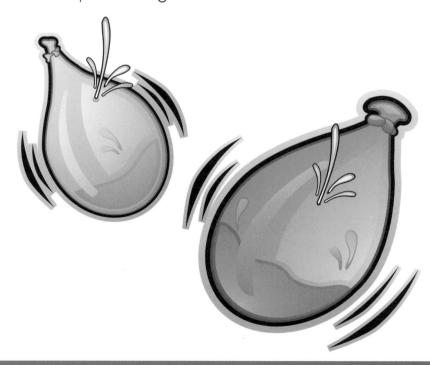

Water Time Bomb

Poke a hole in a balloon before filling it with water. Now the water balloon is a time bomb with a slow leak. Players stand in a circle and toss the balloon around. The object is not to be the one holding the balloon when it runs out of water.

Wrapper Launch

Wrap a foil gum wrapper around your thumb. Leave about a third hanging off. Make a cap on the end by twisting the top of the wrapper on your thumb. Now, take the wrapper off your thumb. Make a fist with a hollow tube inside. Gently push the wrapper cap, hollow-side down, deep into the circle formed by your thumb and index finger. With the flattened palm of your free hand strike the base of your fist with the gum wrapper. The wrapper cap should launch into the air because of the air pressure forced on it by your fist. Get your friends together, enjoy some gum, and have a contest to see who can pop the highest rocket.

Nose Gum

On a large piece of poster board draw a bull's-eye target. Tape the poster board to a clean wall. Give each player a piece of gum to chew for a few minutes. Blindfold one player at a time and spin them around. Instruct the player to take the gum out of his mouth, stick it to his nose, and then try to stick the gum to the target. Whoever gets the closest to the bull's-eye is the winner.

Gum Sculptures

Give each of your friends two or three pieces of bubble gum, an index card, and a toothpick. Let them chew the gum for several minutes. Each player then designs a sculpture with the bubble gum using the toothpick as a tool.

Lost Eyeballs

The lost eyeballs are really marbles! Place the marbles in a medium-size plastic storage container. Fill the container with cooked spaghetti noodles doctored up with a red food coloring and a small amount of cooking oil. Players take turns searching for the lost eyeballs using only their bare feet.

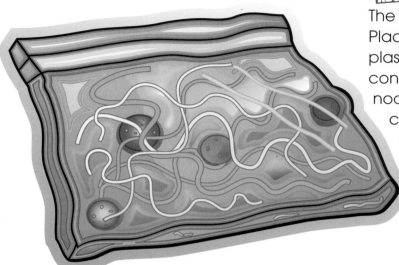

 ## Toe Painting

Instead of finger painting, try toe painting! With adult help and supervision, hang a large piece of paper, white paper tablecloth or even a bed sheet on a wall. Be sure to use a drop cloth, too, if you do this inside the house. Kids dip their toes into pie pans or small plastic containers of different color paints. Watercolors or acrylic paints will work well. Divide your friends into teams and award prizes for the most creative, funniest, and scariest paintings. Have a container of warm soapy water and towels nearby to wash and dry each artist's toes!

 ## Squish Painting

Put a small amount of ketchup and/or mustard inside a large reclosable sandwich or storage bag. Squeeze out the air and tightly seal the bag. Lay the bag flat, and spread the contents evenly. Draw on the bag with your fingers. Smooth over the bag to erase the drawing. What other mixtures can you place in the bag? Try pudding!

Poor Kitty

No one will be able to keep a straight face for very long with this silly game. Everyone sits on the floor in a circle. Choose one friend to be the Poor, Poor Kitty. The Poor, Poor Kitty goes up to another friend in the circle purring and meowing, acting like a cat. The friend must pat the kitty on the head and say, "Poor, Poor Kitty" without laughing. If the player laughs, then he must become the kitty and try to make others around the circle laugh.

Greasy Grimy Gopher Guts Game

Cut out cards on pages 161–167.
Instructions for Play:

Memory Match

Place all cards face down on the table. The object of the game is for a player to collect pairs of cards, matching content and color. To play, players flip two cards at a time. If the cards match content and color, the player removes the pair, sets them aside, and tries to find another matching pair. If the cards do not match, flip the cards face down and it becomes the next player's turn. If a player flips over the spoon, the player flips the spoon face down and rearranges all the remaining cards in play. Play continues until all the cards are removed. The player with the most pairs is the winner.

Not Me Without a Spoon! I

"Great big globs of greasy grimy gopher guts...and me without a spoon!" In this twist on Old Maid, the player WITH the spoon at the end is the winner. Deal all the cards to the players. Each player looks at the cards in their hand and places any pairs face up in front of them. Players take turns drawing a card from another player's hand, and placing any pairs on the table.

Not Me Without a Spoon! 2

Place the spoon card face up in the center of the table. The object of the game is to grab the spoon card after you have collected all the cards of one kind. To play, deal all of the cards to the players. A player offers to trade 1, 2, or 3 cards he or she does not want, in hopes of getting cards of the kind he or she is collecting. Do not say what cards you are collecting. Do not show the cards in trading; keep them face-side down. Simply say, "Trade one, one, one," or "Trade two, two, two," or "Trade three, three, three." All players trade simultaneously—there are no turns! The player who has collected all eight cards quietly grabs the spoon card from the center.

Go Fish!

Deal all of the cards to the players, plus one additional pile—the fishing pool. When all of the players have laid down all of the pairs that they have, the game begins. The first player asks the player to their left for a specific card. In order to ask for a card, you must be holding one of that same content and color. If the person has the card that you asked for, take the card and lay your pair face up on the table. Your turn continues. If the person doesn't have the card that you asked for, then you are told to "Go fish!" and must draw a card from the fishing pool. If you draw the card that you were asking for, you can continue your turn. If you don't draw the card you need, then it is the next person's turn. The game continues until one player has no cards left in his or her hand.

Read, Sing, and Play Along! Gross and Annoying Songs

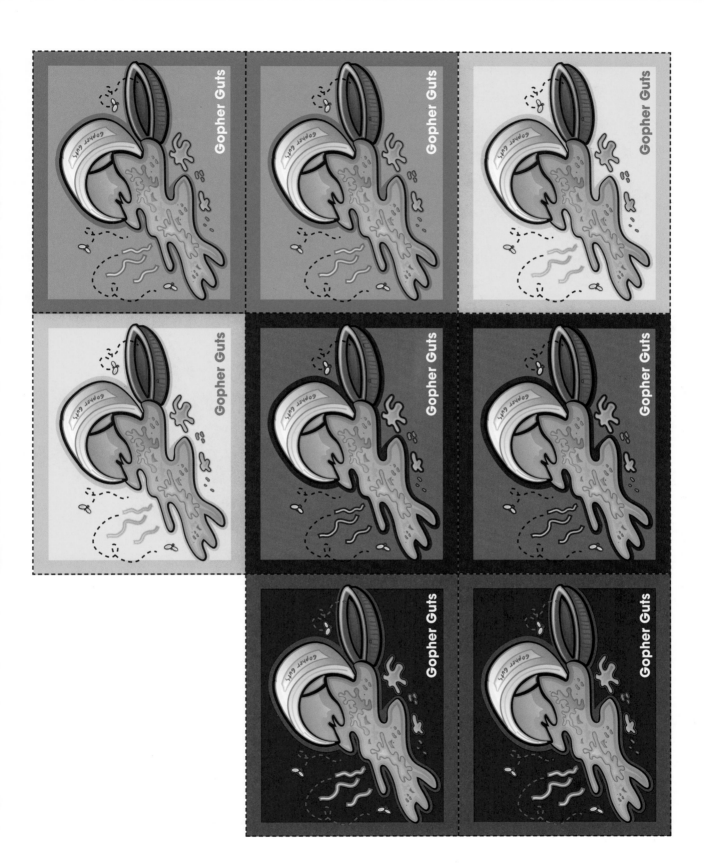

This page was intentionally left blank.

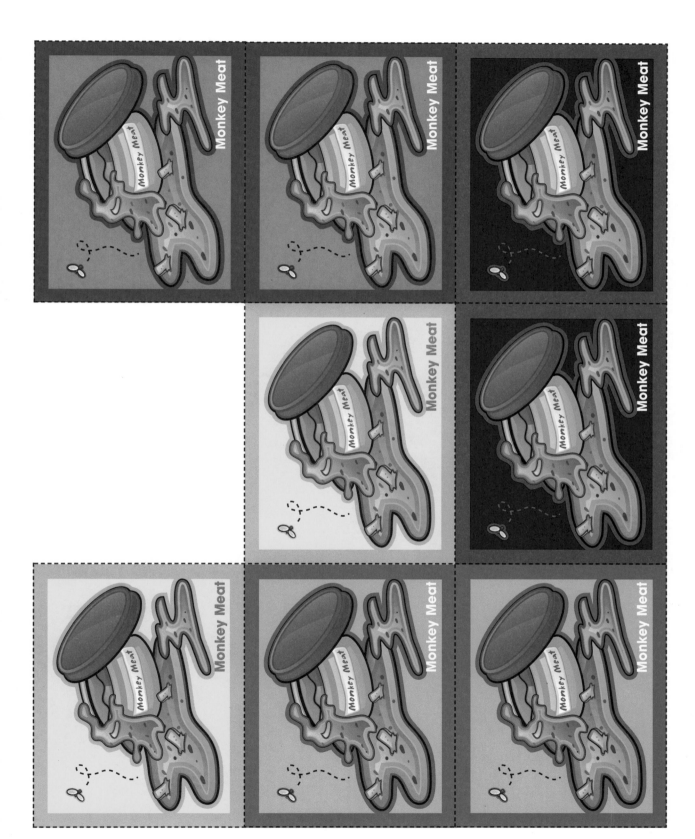

This page was intentionally left blank.

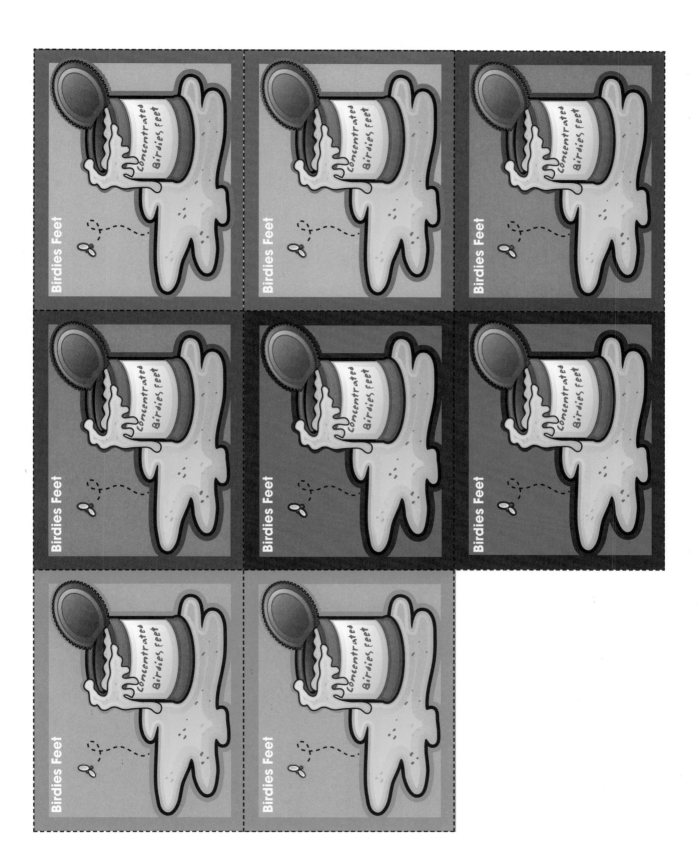

This page was intentionally left blank.

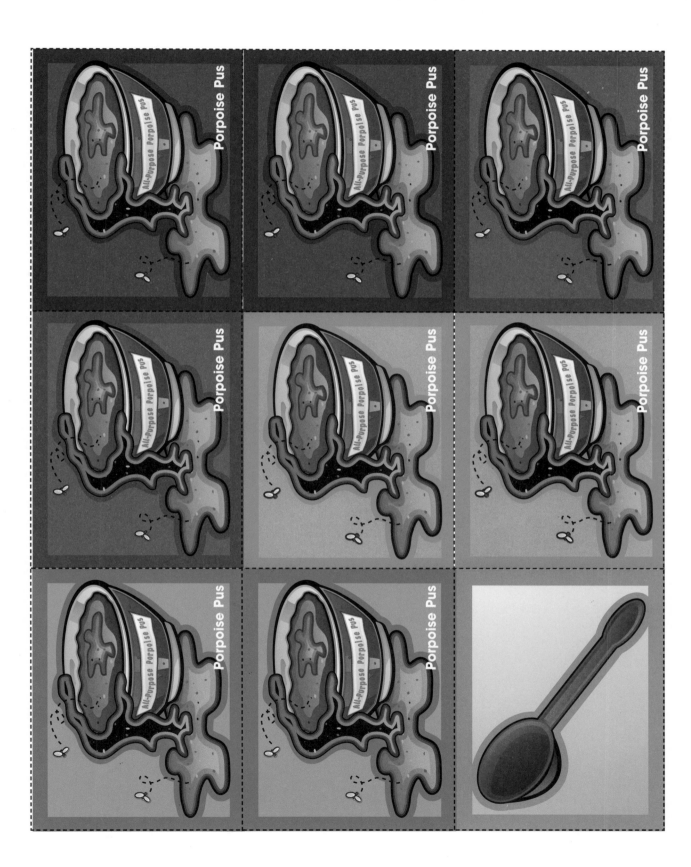

This page was intentionally left blank.

Balloon Orchestra

Everyone in the orchestra holds a balloon. Together, blow up the balloons in unison, pinch the neck closed and let out the air a squeak at a time to the rhythm of some easily recognized song like "Home On The Range" or "Jingle Bells." To end the skit every orchestra member may let go at the director's signal.

Strong Coffee

Set a large pan of dirty water in the center of the stage. You and three of your friends each walk one at a time to the pan, carrying a coffee mug, dip the mug in, bring it up to your lips for a drink, and say:

> *1st friend:* "This coffee is getting worse!"
>
> *2nd friend:* "This tea is getting worse!"
>
> *3rd friend:* "This chocolate is getting worse!"

The fourth friend, walks to pan, dips his hands in and takes out a pair of dirty, wet socks. As he wrings them out he says, "I thought that would get them clean!"

Sucker's Bet

Dare your friends to drink water from a jar through a straw! They're sure to fail with this simple prank.

You'll need:
- Glass jar with a metal lid
- Hammer and Nail
- Drinking straw
- Modeling clay
- Water

Make a hole big enough for the straw in the metal jar lid using a hammer and nail. Fill the jar about halfway with water and replace the lid. Insert a straw through the hole in the lid; then plug the hole up tight with clay around the straw, so that no air can get in. Now, challenge your friend to drink the water in the jar through the straw. Watch how frustrated your friend becomes when the water doesn't budge! By sealing the lid, you've blocked the air pressure and the water can't rise.

The Lawnmower

(One friend is on his hands and knees pretending to be a lawnmower.)

Owner: *(Yanking imaginary rope, while mower sputters)* This old mower, I can't get it going. I need some help. *(Gets help from another friend.)*

Helper #1: So you just want me to yank on this rope, and get it started? That's easy! *(Yanking rope)*

Lawnmower: *(Sputters, bobs up and down)*

Helper #1: I'm sorry. I can't seem to do it. Have you checked the gas?

Owner: Yes, I have. Thanks anyway. Well, let's see who else has a strong arm. *(Selects another friend.)* What I need you to do is to give a real good yank on the starting rope and make it run.

Helper #2: Sure thing. *(Yanks rope a couple of times.)*

Lawnmower: *(Bobs up and down, sputters, coughs)*

Helper #2: Sorry, I can't do it either.

Owner: What I need is someone big and strong. *(Select another person and get him to pull the rope)*

Mower: *(Splutters, coughs, begins to vibrate and run)*

Owner: There. All it needed was a real jerk.

The Important Papers

The setting can be either a king or a boss in his office who instructs an assistant to bring royal or important papers. Your friend runs in with a stack of papers. The king or boss is quite upset, tosses the papers aside, and demands that the assistant bring him his really important papers. Other people bring in other stacks of papers one at a time. The king throws them aside and becomes more and more upset, angrily insisting that he have his important papers. At last someone comes in with a roll of bathroom tissue. The king knights or the boss promotes the assistant, thanking him profusely before running off the stage in visible relief.

Let One Rip!

Place a book or dollar bill out in the open. Wait for someone to come over and pick it up. When the person bends over, rip a piece of cloth. How many people will reach back to see if their clothing ripped?

The Little Green Ball

The first friend enters and says, "Oh, no. I've lost it!" He then starts to search around on the floor. The second friend comes in and asks what the first person is looking for. The first person replies that he has lost his little green ball. Both continue searching the floor. Several more friends come on and are told about the lost little green ball. Even members of the audience can be persuaded to join in the search. The key is to be melodramatic, exaggerating movements and words. After enough time has been dragged out, the first person sticks a finger up his nose and says, "Don't worry! I can make another one!" YUK!!!!!

The Legend of Herbert Smear...

Tell ghost stories in the dark and pass around the bowls of the items below. Another option is to blindfold your friends, have them sit in a circle on the floor, and pass the body parts around the circle for each to feel as you tell the horrific tale.

Brains: An overcooked head of cauliflower

 **Eyes:** Olives or peeled grapes

Live Worms: Gummi worms—not as scary though

 **Intestines:** Soggy marshmallows, strung together

Zombie Hair: Dried corn silk from ears of corn

Barf/Vomit: Chunky salsa and canned corn mixed together

Decaying Flesh: Mashed potatoes topped with instant potato flakes, add coloring

Veins: Cooked spaghetti

Teeth: Dried popcorn kernels

 **Maggots:** Cooked mini pasta shells, or rice

Breaking Bones: Fresh crisp celery or dog biscuits

Scrambled Brains: Lumpy cottage cheese

Glass of Water

Place a glass of water in the middle of the stage. The first friend crawls across the floor crying for water, but dies dramatically shortly after beginning his crawl. The second friend dies just short of the glass of water. The third friend on his last bit of strength really hams up his thirst and desperation as much as possible. But reaching the water, he takes out a comb, grooms his hair with the water, sighs with relief, and goes off stage.

Puppy in the Box

Props: A cardboard box, and a stuffed dog or animal.

Announcer: This scene takes place on the street outside a grocery store. *(Several friends are gathered, chatting outside the store.)*

Michael: *(Enters holding the box)* Hi guys! Would you please hold this box for me while I go into the store? *(Exits)*

Nathan: I wonder what's in the box?

Jason: I don't know, but something yellow is leaking out!

Bob: *(Rubs finger against the bottom of box then licks finger.)* Hmmm, it tastes like lemon soda.

Nathan: *(Also rubs box and licks finger.)* No. I think it's more like chicken soup.

Michael: *(Returns, looks into the box.)* Oh, you naughty puppy!

THIS END UP

Arctic Cereal

Tomorrow's breakfast will be unforgettable with this simple, harmless prank. The night before, take half a bowl of cereal and put milk over it. Put it into the freezer. In the morning, take the bowl out, cover it the rest of the way with more cereal and milk, and serve!

Ooooo, Yuck!

Wet your hand with water, pretend to sneeze, and sprinkle the water on someone. Here's another gross one: Look at your friend and say, "Oh my gosh! What's that hanging out of your nose?"

Cool Drinks

Dissolve a package of flavored gelatin according to the directions on the box. Pour the liquid gelatin into drinking glasses, and place a plastic straw in each. Set the glasses on a tray in the refrigerator until the gelatin firms up. Serve the cool beverages to your friends or family ... watch them try to drink 'em up!

Confetti Shower

Make confetti by tearing scrap paper into very small pieces. Place confetti into someone's umbrella and then close it and wait for the next rain. Or put the confetti in a coffee mug and pretend to trip, spilling the coffee on an unsuspecting victim. Be a good sport and clean up your mess!

Jokes

1. Why did the toilet paper roll down the hill?
    Because it wanted to get to the bottom!

2. How do you make a snake cry?
    Take away its rattle!

3. What monkey can fly?
    A hot air baboon!

4. What happened to the mouse who fell into a glass of soda?
    Nothing, it was a soft drink!

5. Why did the firefly get bad grades in school?
    He wasn't very bright!

6. Why do birds fly south?
    It's too far to walk!

7. Why did the boy bring toilet paper to the birthday party?
    Because he's a party pooper!

8. What's worse than finding a worm in your apple?
    Finding half a worm!

9. What is a dog's favorite snack?
    Pupcorn

10. Why don't elephants pick their nose?
    They don't know where to hide a 30-pound booger!

11. Why did the booger cross the road?
    Because he was tired of getting picked on.

12. How do you count cows?
    With a cowculator!

13. Why did the fish cross the river?
    To get to its school!

14. What did the chicken say to the farmer?
    Nothing! A chicken can't talk!

15. What is a volcano?
    A mountain with hiccups!

Read, Sing, and Play Along! Gross and Annoying Songs

16. Why does a hummingbird hum?
It doesn't know the words!

17. Why does a gorilla have big nostrils?
Because it has big fingers!

18. Why didn't the skeleton cross the road?
Because he had no body to go with!

19. Where do you find a dog with no legs?
Right where you left him!

20. What is Beethoven doing in his grave?
Decomposing!

21. What do you call two spiders who just got married?
Newlywebs!

22. What does a crab use to call someone?
A shellular phone!

23. What is the difference between boogers & broccoli?
Kids don't eat broccoli

24. What do rabbits do when they get married?
Go on a bunnymoon

25. How do you make a tissue dance?
Put a little boogie in it!

26. Why did the chicken cross the playground?
To get to the other slide.

27. What do you call a sleeping bull?
A bulldozer!

28. My friend is built upside down...
His nose runs, and his feet smell!

29. What is the best thing to take into the desert?
A thirst aid kit!

30. What do you call a fish without an eye?
A Fsh!

31. What is black and white, black and white, and green?
Two skunks fighting over a pickle!

32. How do birds get in shape?
They do worm-ups!

33. Where does a spider look for new words?
In the Webster's dictionary

34. If everyone in the country drove a pink automobile, what would we be?
A pink carnation!

35. Which side of the chicken do the feathers grow on?
The outside!

36. What did the snake give to his girlfriend on their first date?
A good night hiss!

37. Doctor, Doctor... What did the x-ray of my head show?
Nothing.

38. What do you call a monkey holding a firecracker?
A baboom!

39. What did one firefly say to the other before he left?
Bye! I'm glowing now!

40. Doctor, Doctor... did you hear about the boy who swallowed a quarter?
There's no change yet.

41. What did the cat eat for breakfast?
Mice Crispies

42. Why was the father centipede so upset?
All of the kids needed new shoes!

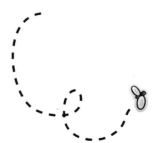

43. What did the dog say when he sat on sandpaper?
Rufffff

44. What do you call a pony with a sore throat?
A little horse!

45. What pet makes the loudest noise?
A trum-pet!

46. What did the teddy bear say when the monkey offered him dessert?
No thanks, I'm stuffed.

47. How do bees travel
They take the buzz!

48. How does a dog smell?
Badly!

49. Why are frogs good outfielders?
Because they can catch lots of flies.

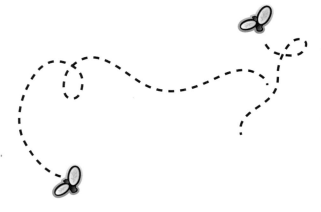

50. How do you make a witch itch?
Take away her W.

51. Why did the gum cross the road?
Because it was stuck to the chicken's foot!

52. Why did the tomato blush?
Because it saw the salad dressing!

53. What does a dentist call his x-rays?
Tooth-pics!

54. What do you get when you cross a bird, a car, and a dog?
A flying car-pet

55. How come a cheetah can't play hide and seek?
Because he's already been spotted.

56. What has four wheels and flies?
A garbage truck!

57. Why did the turkey cross the road?
To prove that he wasn't chicken!

58. What invention enables man to walk through walls?
A door.

59. What did the math book say to the other math book?
"I've got problems."

60. Where do snowmen go to dance?
A snowball!

Sheet Music and Lyrics

Read, Sing, and Play Along! Gross and Annoying Songs **179**

Camp Spaghetti

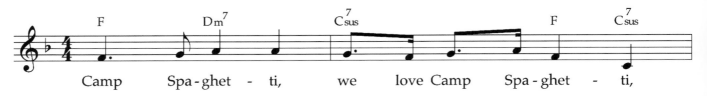

Camp   Spa-ghet - ti,   we   love Camp   Spa - ghet - ti,

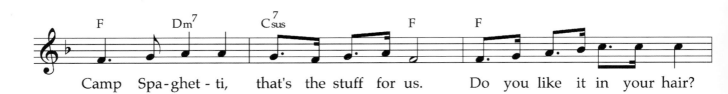

Camp   Spa-ghet - ti,   that's the stuff for us.   Do you like it in your hair?

Yes,   we like   it in   our hair!   In   your hair?   In   our hair!

In your hair? In our hair! Camp Spa-ghet - ti,   we love Camp Spa-ghet - ti,

Camp   Spa-ghet - ti,   that's   the stuff   for us.

2nd Verse
Do you like it in your pants?
Yes we like it in our pants.
In your pants?
In our pants!
In your pants?
In our pants!
Camp Spaghetti, we love camp
    Spaghetti,
Camp Spaghetti, that's the stuff
    for us.

3rd verse
Do you like it in your nose?
Yes we like it in our nose.
In your nose?
In our nose!
In your nose?
In our nose!
Camp Spaghetti, we love camp
    Spaghetti,
Camp Spaghetti, that's the stuff
    for us.

Soap and Towel

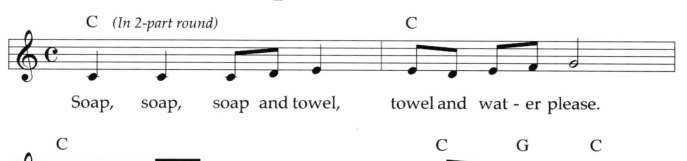

Soap, soap, soap and towel, towel and wat - er please.

Mer - rily, mer - rily, mer - rily, mer - rily, wash your dir - ty knees.

Read, Sing, and Play Along! Gross and Annoying Songs **181**

Be Kind to Your Web-Footed Friends

Be   kind   to your web - foot - ed   friends,   for a

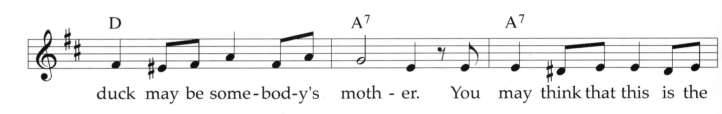

duck   may be some-bod-y's   moth - er.   You   may think that this   is the

end,   but   it's   not!

2nd Verse

Be kind to your web-footed friends,
For a duck may be somebody's
        mother.
You may think that this is the end,
Well, it ain't!

3rd Verse

Be kind to your web-footed friends,
For a duck may be somebody's
        mother.
You may think that this is the end,
And it is!

This Old Man

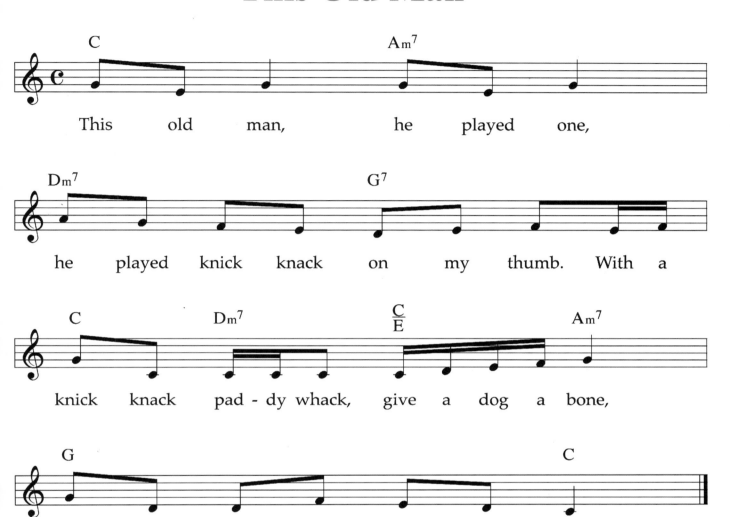

This old man, he played one,
he played knick knack on my thumb. With a
knick knack pad - dy whack, give a dog a bone,
this old man came rol - ling home.

2nd Verse
This old man, he played two,
He played knick knack on my shoe.
With a knick knack paddywhack,
   give a dog a bone,
This old man came rolling home.

3rd Verse
This old man, he played three,
He played knick knack on my knee.
With a knick knack paddywhack,
   give a dog a bone,
This old man came rolling home.

This Old Man (continued)

4th Verse
This old man, he played four,
He played knick knack on my door.
With a knick knack paddywhack,
    give a dog a bone,
This old man came rolling home.

5th Verse
This old man, he played five,
He played knick knack on my hive.
With a knick knack paddywhack,
    give a dog a bone,
This old man came rolling home.

6th Verse
This old man, he played six,
He played knick knack on my sticks.
With a knick knack paddywhack,
    give a dog a bone,
This old man came rolling home.

7th Verse
This old man, he played seven,
He played knick knack up in heaven.
With a knick knack paddywhack,
    give a dog a bone,
This old man came rolling home.

8th Verse
This old man, he played eight,
He played knick knack on my gate.
With a knick knack paddywhack,
    give a dog a bone,
This old man came rolling home.

9th Verse
This old man, he played nine,
He played knick knack on my spine.
With a knick knack paddywhack,
    give a dog a bone,
This old man came rolling home.

10th Verse
This old man, he played ten,
He played knick knack once again.
With a knick knack paddywhack,
    give a dog a bone,
This old man came rolling home.

We're Here Because We're Here

Read, Sing, and Play Along! Gross and Annoying Songs

Apples and Bananas

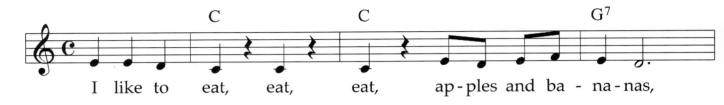

I like to eat, eat, eat, ap-ples and ba - na - nas,

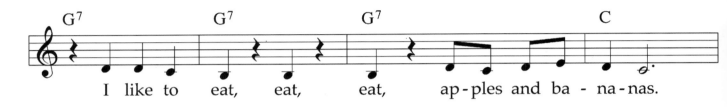

I like to eat, eat, eat, ap-ples and ba - na - nas.

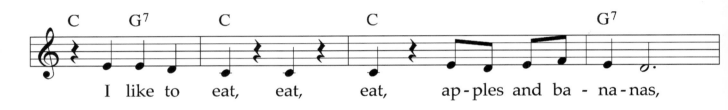

I like to eat, eat, eat, ap-ples and ba - na - nas,

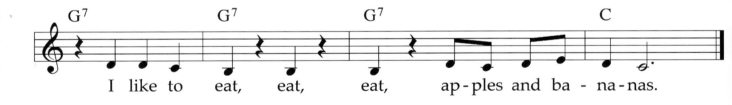

I like to eat, eat, eat, ap-ples and ba - na - nas.

2nd Verse
I like to ate, ate, ate ay-ples and ba-nay-nays,
I like to ate, ate, ate ay-ples and ba-nay-nays.
I like to ate, ate, ate ay-ples and ba-nay-nays,
I like to ate, ate, ate ay-ples and ba-nay-nays.

Apples and Bananas (continued)

3rd Verse

I like to eat, eat, eat ee-ples and bee-nee-nees,
I like to eat, eat, eat ee-ples and bee-nee-nees.
I like to eat, eat, eat ee-ples and bee-nee-nees,
I like to eat, eat, eat ee-ples and bee-nee-nees.

4th Verse

I like to ite, ite, ite i-ples and bi-ni-nies,
I like to ite, ite, ite i-ples and bi-ni-nies.
I like to ite, ite, ite i-ples and bi-ni-nies,
I like to ite, ite, ite i-ples and bi-ni-nies.

5th Verse

I like to ote, ote, ote oh-ples and bo-no-nos,
I like to ote, ote, ote oh-ples and bo-no-nos.
I like to ote, ote, ote oh-ples and bo-no-nos,
I like to ote, ote, ote oh-ples and bo-no-nos.

6th Verse

I like to oot, oot, oot oo-ples and boo-noo-noos,
I like to oot, oot, oot oo-ples and boo-noo-noos.
I like to oot, oot, oot oo-ples and boo-noo-noos,
I like to oot, oot, oot oo-ples and boo-noo-noos.

Oh, You Can't Get To Heaven

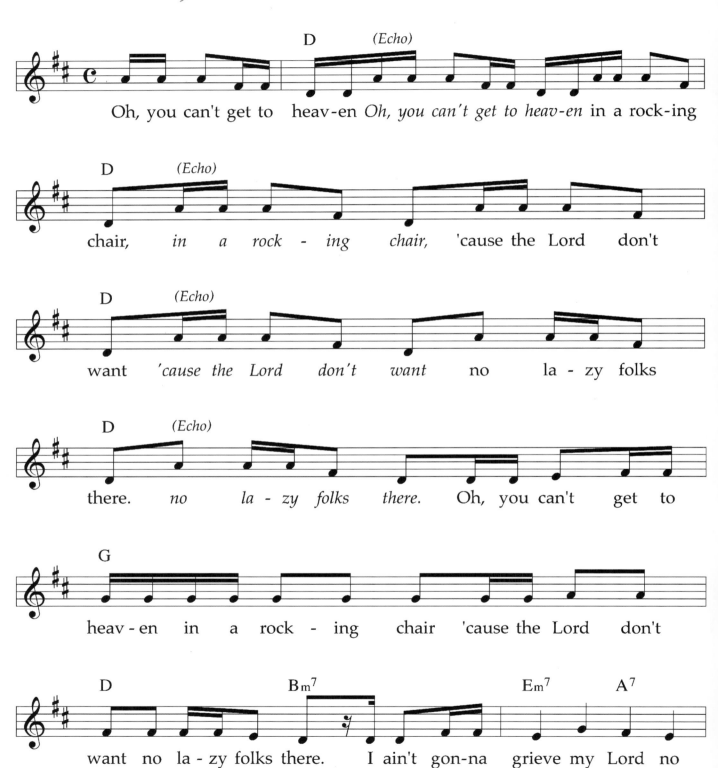

more.   I ain't gon-na   grieve my Lord no more, I ain't gon-na

grieve my Lord no more,   I ain't gon-na   grieve my Lord no

more.

2nd Verse
Oh, you can't get to heaven
(Oh, you can't get to heaven)
On roller skates,
(On roller skates,)
'Cause you'd roll right by
('Cause you'd roll right by)
Those pearly gates.
(Those pearly gates.)
Oh, you can't get to heaven on roller skates
'Cause you'd roll right by those pearly gates.
I ain't gonna grieve my Lord no more.

I ain't gonna grieve my Lord no more,
I ain't gonna grieve my Lord no more,
I ain't gonna grieve my Lord no more.

On Top of My Pizza

C   F   C   F

drink.   I looked in the sauce

C

pan   right un - der the lid,

Am7   G

—   no mat - ter where I   looked   those

G7sus   C

mush-rooms stayed hid.   Next time you make

F   C

piz - za,   I'm beg-ging you, please,

Am7   G

—   do not give me mush - rooms,

—   but just plain old cheese.

The Worm Song

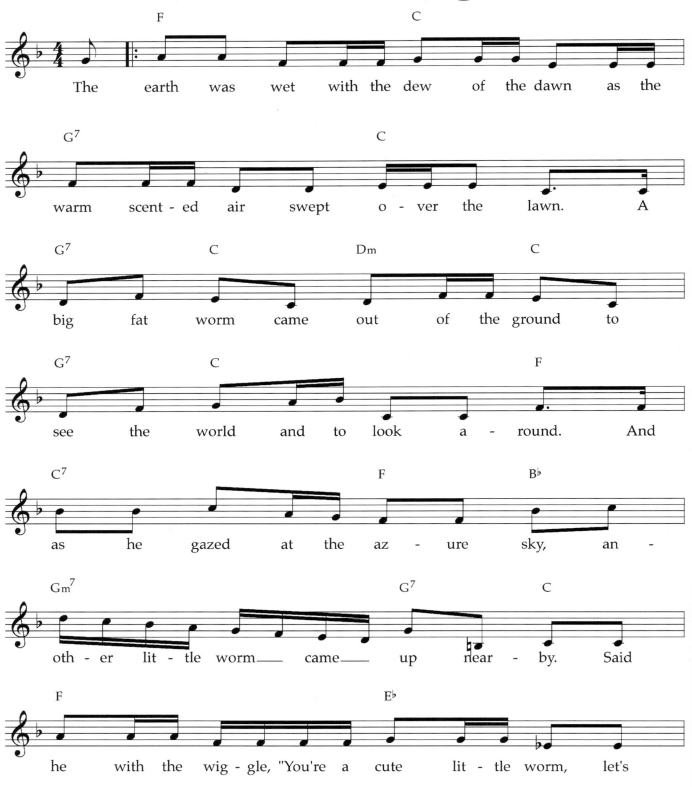

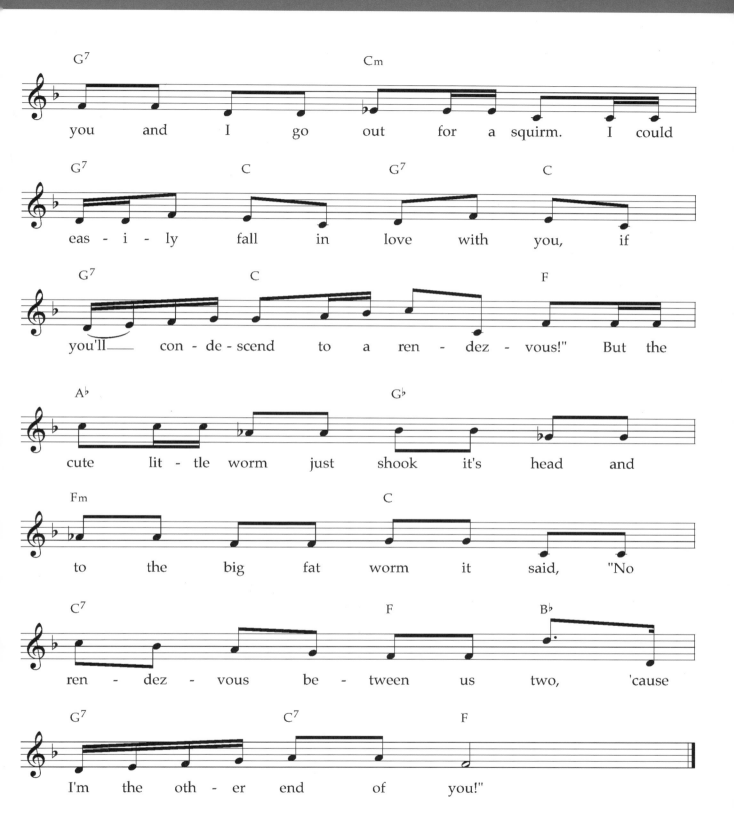

Little Black Things

Lit - tle   black   things,   lit - tle   black   things,   run - ning

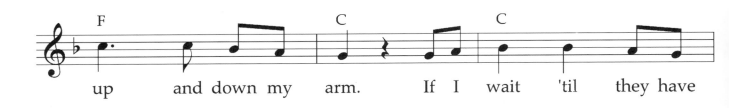

up   and down my   arm.   If   I   wait   'til   they have

ba - bies   I   can   start   a   black thing   farm.

2nd Verse

Haven't had a bath in two years and I never wash my clothes.
'Cause I got these little black things—where they came from no one knows!

Little black things, little black things, running up and down my arm.
If I wait 'til they have babies I can start a black thing farm.

3rd Verse

Had a boyfriend, tried to kiss me, but he turned and gave a yell.
And I never got to ask him was it the black things or the smell?

Little black things, little black things, running up and down my arm.
If I wait 'til they have babies I can start a black thing farm.

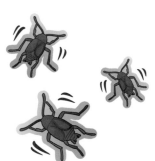

Ta Ra Ra Boom De Ay

Ta Ra Ra Boom De Ay —— Ta Ra Ra Boom De Ay —— Ta Ra Ra

Boom De Ay —— Ta Ra Ra Boom De Ay —— Ta Ra Ra

Boom De Ay —— Ta Ra Ra Boom De Ay —— Ta Ra Ra

Boom De Ay —— Ta Ra Ra Boom De Ay

Read, Sing, and Play Along! Gross and Annoying Songs

Three Cheers for the Bus Driver

Three— cheers— for the bus driv-er, the bus driv-er, the

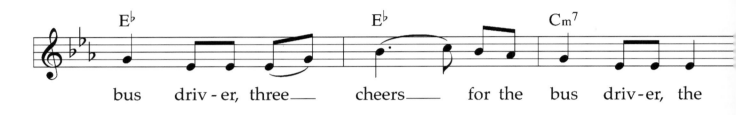

bus driv-er, three— cheers— for the bus driv-er, the

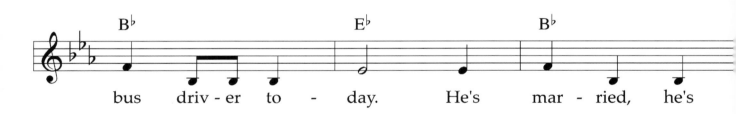

bus driv-er to - day. He's mar - ried, he's

jol - ly, he's built like a trol - ley. Three— cheers— for the

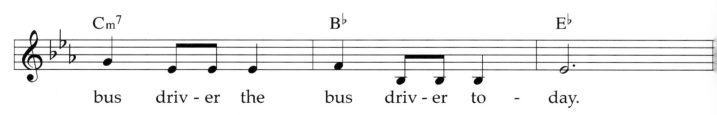

bus driv-er the bus driv-er to - day.

2nd Verse
Three cheers for the bus driver, the bus driver, the bus driver,
Three cheers for the bus driver, the bus driver today.
God bless him—he needs it! God bless him—he needs it!
Three cheers for the bus driver, the bus driver today.

There Was a Little Rooster

Oh, there was a lit-tle roos-ter in our lit-tle coun-try store, and he phfft! on the count-er and he phfft! on the floor, and he phfft! on the su-gar and he phfft! on the bread, and if I had-n't ducked he'd have phfft! on my head.

Read, Sing, and Play Along! Gross and Annoying Songs

An Annoying Song

I know a song that gets on ev' - ry-bod - y's nerves.

I know a song that gets on ev' - ry-bod - y's nerves.

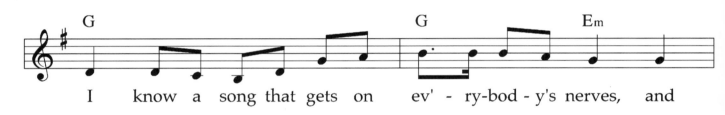

I know a song that gets on ev' - ry-bod - y's nerves, and

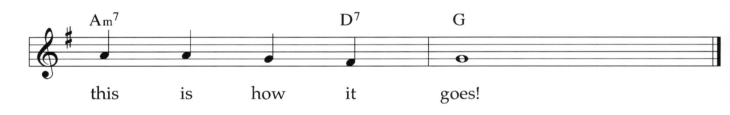

this is how it goes!

Polly Wolly Doodle

Oh, I went down South for to see my Sal, sing
Pol-ly Wol-ly Doo-dle all the day. My— Sal, she is a
spunk-y gal, sing Pol-ly Wol-ly Doo-dle all the day. Fare thee
well, fare the well, fare thee well my fair-y
fay, for I'm goin' to Lou'-si-an-a for to
see my Su-sy-an-a, sing Pol-ly Wol-ly Doo-dle all the day.

Read, Sing, and Play Along! Gross and Annoying Songs

Polly Wolly Doodle (continued)

2nd Verse
Oh, my Sal, she is a maiden fair,
Sing Polly Wolly Doodle all the day
With curly eyes and laughing hair,
Sing Polly Wolly Doodle all the day.

Fare thee well, fare thee well, fare thee well my fairy fay,
For I'm going to Lou'siana for to see my Susyana,
Sing Polly Wolly Doodle all the day.

Take Me Out of This Camp, Please

Read, Sing, and Play Along! Gross and Annoying Songs

Black Socks

Black socks, they nev - er get dir - ty, the
long - er you wear them the strong - er they get.
Some - times I think of the laun - dry, but
some - thing keeps tell - ing me, don't wash them yet.

My Bonnie Lies Over the Ocean

My Bon - nie lies o - ver the o - cean,_____ my

Bon - nie lies o - ver the sea,_____ my Bon - nie lies o - ver the

o - cean,_____ oh, bring back my Bon - nie to me.

Bring back, bring back, bring back my Bon - nie to me._____

Bring back, bring back, bring back my Bon - nie to me.

Read, Sing, and Play Along! Gross and Annoying Songs **203**

My Bonnie Lies Over the Ocean (continued)

2nd Verse

Last night as I lay on my pillow,
Last night as I lay on my bed,
Last night as I lay on my pillow,
I dreamed that my Bonnie was dead.

Bring back, bring back,
Bring back my Bonnie to me.
Bring back, bring back,
Bring back my Bonnie to me.

3rd Verse

Oh, blow ye the winds o'er the ocean,
Oh, blow ye the winds o'er the sea,
Oh, blow ye the winds o'er the ocean,
And bring back my Bonnie to me.

Bring back, bring back,
Bring back my Bonnie to me.
Bring back, bring back,
Bring back my Bonnie to me.

4th Verse

The winds have blown over the ocean,
The winds have blown over the sea,
The winds have blown over the ocean,
And brought back my Bonnie to me.

Bring back, bring back,
Bring back my Bonnie to me.
Bring back, bring back,
Bring back my Bonnie to me.

Rueben, Rueben, I've Been Thinking

Rue - ben, Rue - ben, I've been think - ing,

what a sil - ly world this would be,

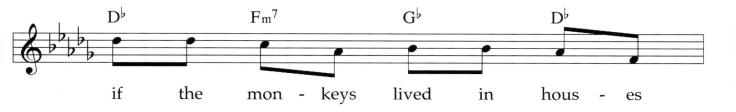

if the mon - keys lived in hous - es

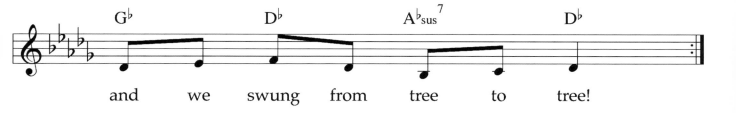

and we swung from tree to tree!

Read, Sing, and Play Along! Gross and Annoying Songs

Reuben, Reuben I've Been Thinking (continued)

2nd Verse
Got a dog, his name is Rover.
He's a very clever pup.
He will stand up on his hind legs
if you hold his front legs up!

3rd Verse
Reuben, Reuben, I've been thinking,
what a silly world this would be,
If jet planes lived in apartments
and we flew across the sea!

4th Verse
There's no need to light a nightlight
on a light night like tonight.
For a nightlight's light is slight light
when the moonlight's white and bright!

Rise and Shine

The   Lord said   to No-ah, there's   gon-na be___ a flood-y, flood-y.

Lord said   to No-ah,   there's   gon-na be___   a flood-y, flood-y.

Get   those   child - ren   out   of   the mud - dy,   mud - dy,

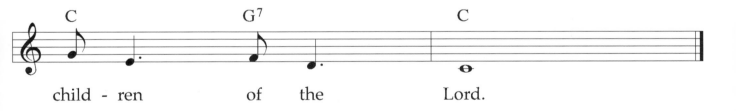

child - ren   of   the   Lord.

Read, Sing, and Play Along! Gross and Annoying Songs **207**

Rise and Shine (continued)

2nd Verse
The Lord told Noah to build Him an arky, arky.
Lord told Noah to build Him an arky, arky.
Build it out of gopher barky, barky, children of the Lord!

3rd Verse
It rained and it poured for forty long daysies, daysies.
Rained and it poured for forty long daysies, daysies.
Almost drove those animals crazies, crazies, children of the Lord!

4th Verse
The sun came out and it dried up the landy, landy.
Sun came out and it dried up the landy, landy.
Everything was fine and dandy, dandy, children of the Lord!

5th Verse
So rise and shine and give God the glory, glory.
Rise and shine and give God the glory, glory.
Rise and shine and give God the glory, glory children of the Lord!

Everywhere That We Go

Read, Sing, and Play Along! Gross and Annoying Songs **209**

might-y might-y Bos - ton!" *might - y might - y Bos - ton!"* And

if they can't hear us, *And if they can't hear us* we

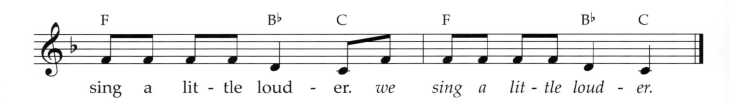

sing a lit - tle loud - er. *we sing a lit - tle loud - er.*

2nd Verse
Everywhere that we go,
(Everywhere that we go,)
People always ask us
(People always ask us)
Who we are
(Who we are)
And where do we come from.
(And where do we come from.)
So we tell them,
(So we tell them,)
"We're from London,
("We're from London,)
Mighty, mighty London!"
(Mighty, mighty London!")
And if they can't hear us,
(And if they can't hear us,)
We sing a little louder.
(We sing a little louder.)

3rd Verse
… "We're from Rio,
("We're from Rio,)
Mighty, mighty Rio!"
(Mighty, mighty Rio!")…

4th Verse
… "We're from Paris,
("We're from Paris,)
Mighty, mighty Paris!"
(Mighty, mighty Paris!")…

5th Verse
… "We're from Hong Kong,
("We're from Hong Kong,)
Mighty, mighty Hong Kong!"
(Mighty, mighty Hong Kong!")…

6th Verse
… "We're from Sidney,
("We're from Sidney,)
Mighty, mighty Sidney!"
(Mighty, mighty Sidney!")
And if they can't hear us—
they're deaf!

We're Five Miles From Camp

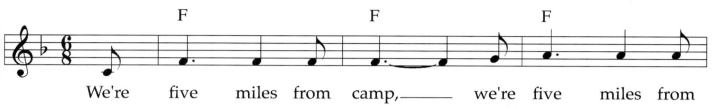

We're five miles from camp,——— we're five miles from

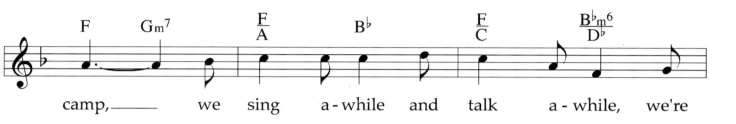

camp,——— we sing a-while and talk a-while, we're

four miles from camp.

2nd Verse
We're four miles from camp,
We're four miles from camp,
We sing awhile and talk awhile,
We're three miles from camp.

3rd Verse
We're three miles from camp,
We're three miles from camp,
We sing awhile and talk awhile,
We're two miles from camp.

4th Verse
We're two miles from camp,
We're two miles from camp,
We sing awhile and talk awhile,
We're one mile from camp.

5th Verse
We're one mile from camp,
We're one mile from camp,
We sing awhile and talk awhile,
And now we're at camp.

La Cucaracha

A Hundred Bottles of Pop

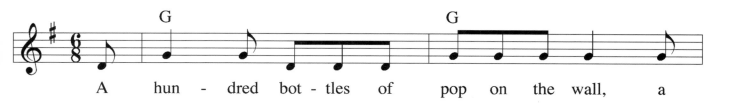

A hun - dred bot - tles of pop on the wall, a

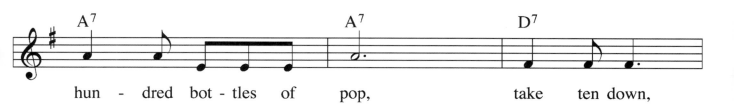

hun - dred bot - tles of pop, take ten down,

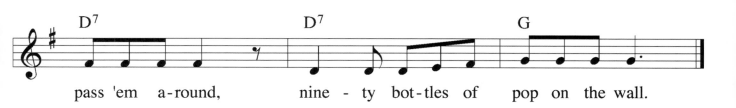

pass 'em a-round, nine - ty bot-tles of pop on the wall.

2nd Verse
Ninety bottles of pop on the wall,
Ninety bottles of pop,
Take ten down and pass 'em around,
Eighty bottles of pop on the wall.

3rd Verse
Eighty bottles of pop on the wall,
Eighty bottles of pop,
Take ten down and pass 'em around,
Seventy bottles of pop on the wall.

Read, Sing, and Play Along! Gross and Annoying Songs

A Hundred Bottles of Pop (continued)

4th Verse
Seventy bottles of pop on the wall,
Seventy bottles of pop,
Take ten down and pass 'em around,
Sixty bottles of pop on the wall.

5th Verse
Sixty bottles of pop on the wall,
Sixty bottles of pop,
Take ten down and pass 'em around,
Fifty bottles of pop on the wall.

6th Verse
Fifty bottles of pop on the wall,
Fifty bottles of pop,
Take ten down and pass 'em around,
Forty bottles of pop on the wall.

7th Verse
Forty bottles of pop on the wall,
Forty bottles of pop,
Take ten down and pass 'em around,
Thirty bottles of pop on the wall.

8th Verse
Thirty bottles of pop on the wall,
Thirty bottles of pop,
Take ten down and pass 'em around,
Twenty bottles of pop on the wall.

9th Verse
Twenty bottles of pop on the wall,
Twenty bottles of pop,
Take ten down and pass 'em around,
Ten bottles of pop on the wall.

10th Verse
Ten bottles of pop on the wall,
Ten bottles of pop,
Take ten down and pass 'em around,
No more bottles of pop on the wall!

Oats, Peas, Beans, and Barley Grow

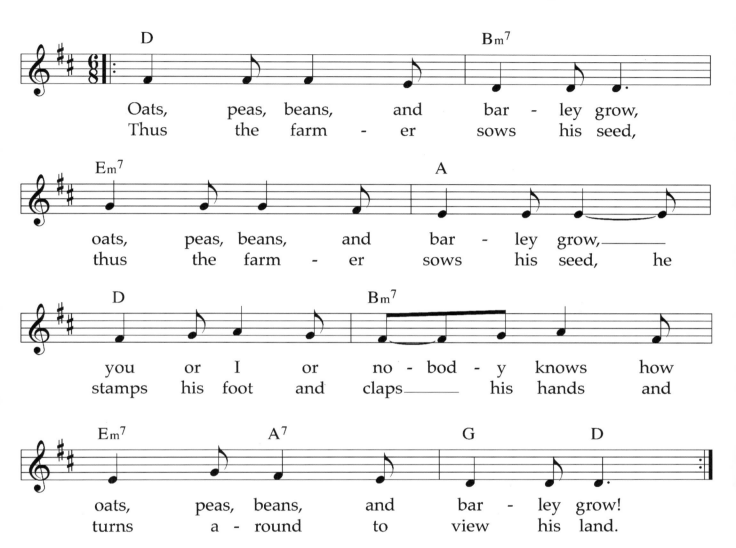

Oats, peas, beans, and bar - ley grow,
Thus the farm - er sows his seed,

oats, peas, beans, and bar - ley grow,—
thus the farm - er sows his seed, he

you or I or no - bod - y knows how
stamps his foot and claps— his hands and

oats, peas, beans, and bar - ley grow!
turns a - round to view his land.

Mary Had a Swarm of Bees

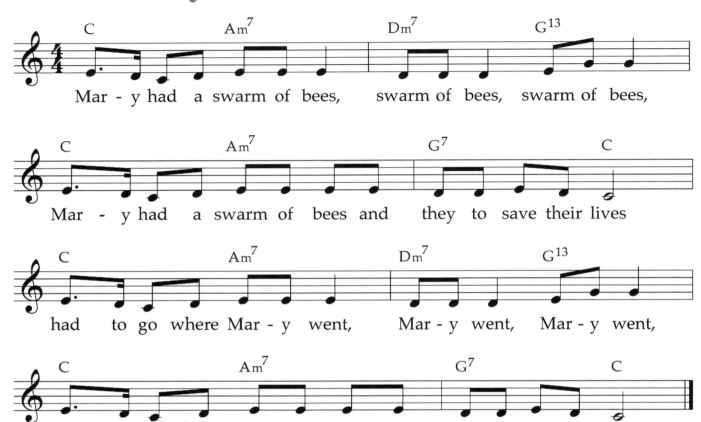

Mar - y had a swarm of bees, swarm of bees, swarm of bees,

Mar - y had a swarm of bees and they to save their lives

had to go where Mar - y went, Mar - y went, Mar - y went,

had to go where Mar - y went 'cause Mar - y had the hives.

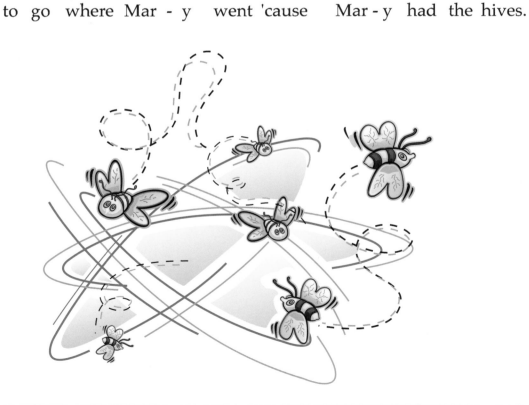

I've Been Workin' on the Railroad

I've been work-in' on the rail-road, all the live long day. I've been work-in' on the rail-road, just to pass the time a-way. Don't you hear the whis-tle blow-in'? Rise up so ear-ly in the morn'. Don't you hear the cap-tain shout-in', "Di-nah, blow your horn!"? Di-nah, won't you blow, Di-nah, won't you blow,

It's Raining, It's Pouring

If You're Happy and You Know It

If you're hap-py and you know it, clap your hands! If you're

hap - py and you know it, clap your hands! If you're

hap-py and you know it then your face will sure-ly show it. If you're

hap - py and you know it, clap your hands!

If You're Happy and You Know It (continued)

2nd Verse

If you're happy and you know it, stomp your feet! *(Stomp)*
If you're happy and you know it, stomp your feet! *(Stomp)*
If you're happy and you know it
Then your face will surely show it.
If you're happy and you know it, stomp your feet! *(Stomp)*

3rd Verse

If you're happy and you know it, shout "Hooray!" *(Shout)*
If you're happy and you know it, shout "Hooray!" *(Shout)*
If you're happy and you know it
Then your face will surely show it.
If you're happy and you know it, shout "Hooray!" *(Shout)*

4th Verse

If you're happy and you know it, do all three! *(Clap, Stomp, and Shout)*
If you're happy and you know it, do all three! *(Clap, Stomp, and Shout)*
If you're happy and you know it
Then your face will surely show it.
If you're happy and you know it, do all three! *(Clap, Stomp, and Shout)*

Michael, Row the Boat Ashore

Mi - chael, row the boat a - shore, Hal - le -

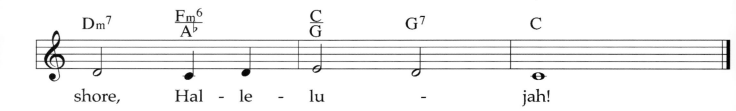

lu - jah! Mi - chael, row the boat a -

shore, Hal - le - lu - jah!

Michael, Row the Boat Ashore (continued)

2nd Verse

My brothers and sisters are all on board, Hallelujah!
My brothers and sisters are all on board, Hallelujah!

Michael, row the boat ashore, Hallelujah!
Michael, row the boat ashore, Hallelujah!

3rd Verse

The river is deep and the river is wide, Hallelujah!
The river is deep and the river is wide, Hallelujah!

Michael, row the boat ashore, Hallelujah!
Michael, row the boat ashore, Hallelujah!

4th Verse

Jordan's river is chilly and cold, Hallelujah!
Jordan's river is chilly and cold, Hallelujah!

Michael, row the boat ashore, Hallelujah!
Michael, row the boat ashore, Hallelujah!

Head, Shoulders, Knees, and Toes

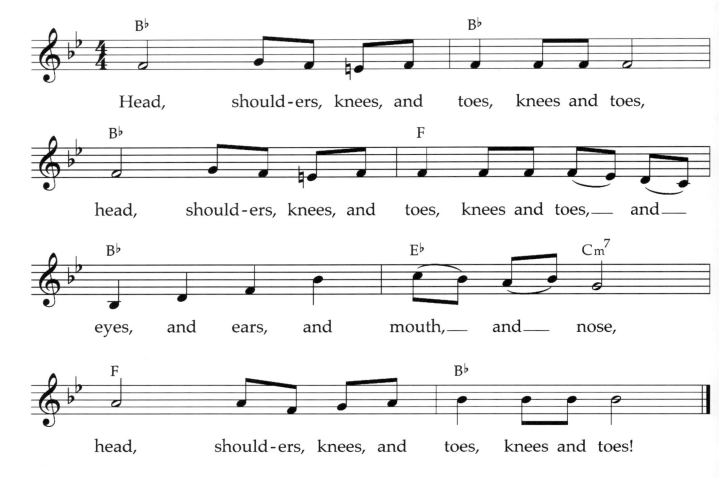

Head, should-ers, knees, and toes, knees and toes,

head, should-ers, knees, and toes, knees and toes,— and—

eyes, and ears, and mouth,— and— nose,

head, should-ers, knees, and toes, knees and toes!

2nd Verse
*, shoulders, knees, and toes, knees and toes,
*, shoulders, knees, and toes, knees and toes,
And eyes, and ears, and mouth, and nose,
*, shoulders, knees, and toes, knees and toes!

3rd Verse
*, *, knees, and toes, knees and toes,
*, *, knees, and toes, knees and toes,
And eyes, and ears, and mouth, and nose,
*, *, knees, and toes, knees and toes!

Head, Shoulders, Knees, and Toes (continued)

4th Verse
*, *, *, and toes, * and toes,
*, *, *, and toes, * and toes,
And eyes, and ears, and mouth, and nose,
*, *, *, and toes, * and toes!

5th Verse
*, *, *, and *, * and *,
*, *, *, and *, * and *,
And eyes, and ears, and mouth, and nose,
*, *, *, and *, * and *!

6th Verse
*, *, *, and *, * and *,
*, *, *, and *, * and *,
And *, and ears, and mouth, and nose,
*, *, *, and *, * and *!

7th Verse
*, *, *, and *, * and *,
*, *, *, and *, * and *,
And *, and *, and mouth, and nose,
*, *, *, and *, * and *!

8th Verse
*, *, *, and *, * and *,
*, *, *, and *, * and *,
And *, and *, and *, and nose,
*, *, *, and *, * and *!

9th Verse
*, *, *, and *, * and *,
*, *, *, and *, * and *,
And *, and *, and *, and *,
*, *, *, and *, * and *!

Read, Sing, and Play Along! Gross and Annoying Songs

Kum Ba Yah

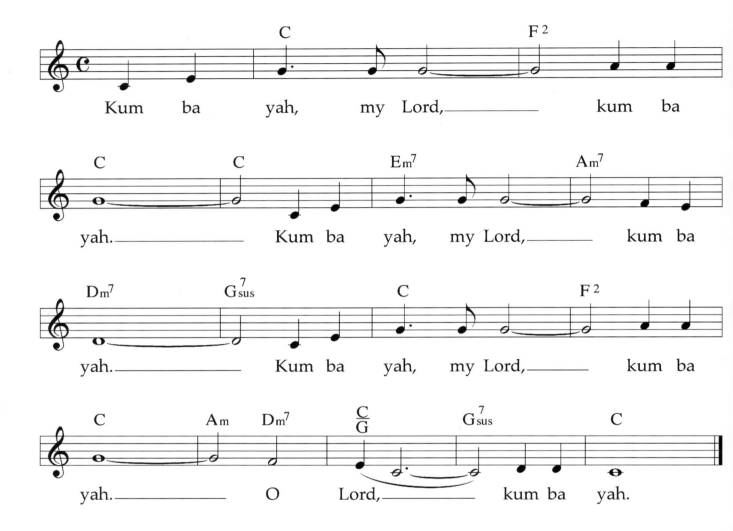

2nd Verse
Someone's singing, Lord, kum ba yah.
Someone's singing, Lord, kum ba yah.
Someone's singing, Lord, kum ba yah.
O, Lord, kum ba yah.

3rd Verse
Someone's praying, Lord, kum ba yah.
Someone's praying, Lord, kum ba yah.
Someone's praying, Lord, kum ba yah.
O, Lord, kum ba yah.

4th Verse
Someone's crying, Lord, kum ba yah.
Someone's crying, Lord, kum ba yah.
Someone's crying, Lord, kum ba yah.
O, Lord, kum ba yah.

The Old Chevrolet

Read, Sing, and Play Along! Gross and Annoying Songs 227

Oh, Playmate,
Come Out and Play With Me

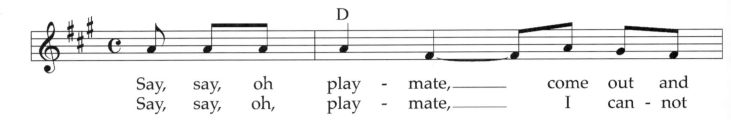

Say, say, oh play - mate,_____ come out and
Say, say, oh, play - mate,_____ I can - not

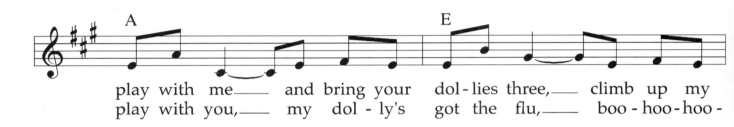

play with me___ and bring your dol - lies three,___ climb up my
play with you,___ my dol - ly's got the flu,___ boo - hoo - hoo -

ap - ple tree,___ shout down my rain barr'l___ slide down my
hoo - hoo - hoo,___ ain't got no rain barr'l,___ ain't got no

cel - lar door,___ and we'll be jol - ly friends___ for - ev - er more.
cel - lar door,___ but we'll be jol - ly friends___ for - ev - er more.

I'm a Nut

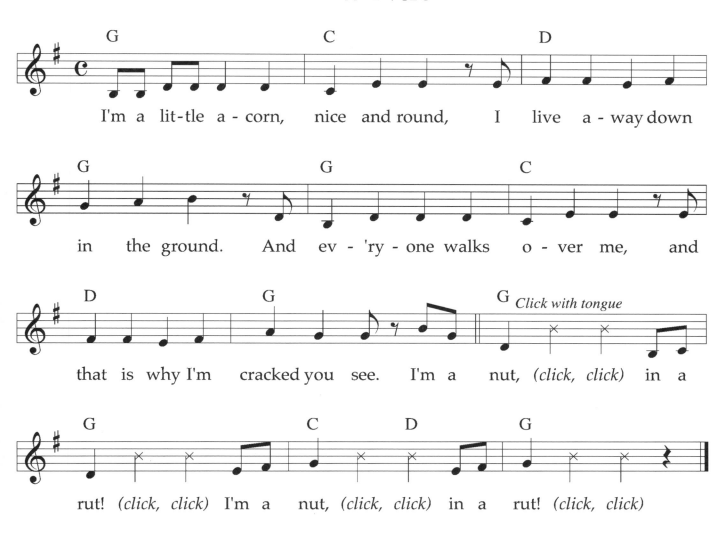

G   C   D

I'm a lit-tle a-corn, nice and round, I live a-way down

G   G   C

in the ground. And ev-'ry-one walks o-ver me, and

D   G   G *Click with tongue*

that is why I'm cracked you see. I'm a nut, *(click, click)* in a

G   C   D   G

rut! *(click, click)* I'm a nut, *(click, click)* in a rut! *(click, click)*

    Read, Sing, and Play Along! Gross and Annoying Songs

Glub, Glub, Glub Your Boat

(In 2-part round)

Glub, glub, glub your boat un - der-neath the stream.

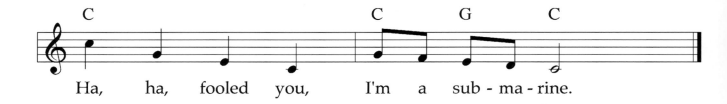

Ha, ha, fooled you, I'm a sub - ma - rine.

Squirty Orange

Oh, I wish I were a lit-tle squir-ty orange, *squir-ty orange*, oh, I

wish I were a lit-tle squir-ty orange, *squir-ty orange*, I'd go

squir-ty, squir-ty, squir-ty o-ver ev-'ry-bo-dy's shir-ty, oh, I

wish I were a lit-tle squir-ty orange, *squir-ty orange!*

2nd Verse
Oh, I wish I were a little bottle of pop,
(Bottle of pop,)
Oh, I wish I were a little bottle of pop,
(Bottle of pop,)
I'd go down with a slurp and come up with a burp,
Oh, I wish I were a little bottle of pop.
(Bottle of pop.)

Read, Sing, and Play Along! Gross and Annoying Songs

Squirty Orange (continued)

3rd Verse
Oh, I wish I were a little foreign car,
(Foreign car,)
Oh, I wish I were a little foreign car,
(Foreign car,)
I'd go speedy, speedy, speedy over ev'rybody's feety,
Oh, I wish I were a little foreign car.
(Foreign car.)

4th Verse
Oh, I wish I were a little mosquito,
(Mosquito,)
Oh, I wish I were a little mosquito,
(Mosquito,)
I'd go hidey, hidey, hidey under ev'rybody's nightie,
Oh, I wish I were a little mosquito.
(Mosquito.)

5th Verse
Oh, I wish I were a little band-aid,
(Band-aid,)
Oh, I wish I were a little band-aid,
(Band-aid,)
I'd stick to the hairs and pull them up in pairs,
Oh, I wish I were a little band-aid.
(Band-aid.)

6th Verse
Oh, I wish I were a little striped skunk,
(Striped skunk,)
Oh, I wish I were a little striped skunk,
(Striped skunk,)
I'd sit up in the trees and perfume all the breeze,
Oh, I wish I were a little striped skunk.
(Striped skunk.)

Greasy Grimy Gopher Guts

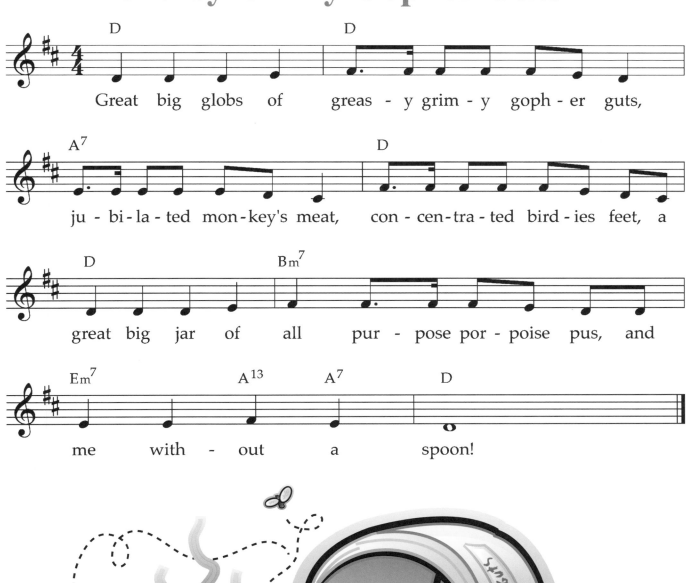

Great big globs of greas - y grim - y goph - er guts,

ju - bi - la - ted mon - key's meat, con - cen - tra - ted bird - ies feet, a

great big jar of all pur - pose por - poise pus, and

me with - out a spoon!

Read, Sing, and Play Along! Gross and Annoying Songs **233**

I Met a Bear

The oth-er day, *The oth-er day,* I met a bear, *I met a bear,* a-way up

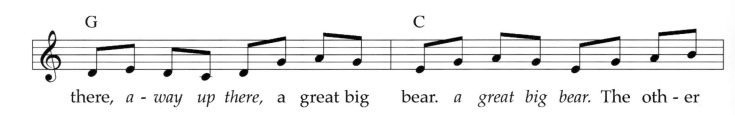

there, *a - way up there,* a great big bear. *a great big bear.* The oth - er

day, I met a bear, a great big bear a - way up there.

2nd Verse
He looked at me.
(He looked at me.)
I looked at him.
(I looked at him.)
He sized up me.
(He sized up me.)
I sized up him.
(I sized up him.)
He looked at me. I looked at him.
He sized up me. I sized up him.

3rd Verse
He said to me,
(He said to me,)
"Why don't you run?
("Why don't you run?)
I see you don't
(I see you don't)
Have any gun."
(Have any gun.")
He said to me "Why don't you run?
I see you don't have any gun."

I Met a Bear (continued)

4th Verse
And so I ran
(And so I ran)
Away from there
(Away from there)
And right behind
(And right behind)
Me was that bear.
(Me was that bear.)
And so I ran away from there
And right behind me was that bear.

5th Verse
Ahead of me,
(Ahead of me,)
I saw a tree,
(I saw a tree,)
A great big tree,
(A great big tree,)
Oh, golly gee.
(Oh, golly gee.)
Ahead of me I saw a tree
A great big tree, oh, golly gee.

6th Verse
The lowest branch
(The lowest branch)
Was 10 feet up.
(Was 10 feet up.)
I had to jump
(I had to jump)
And trust my luck.
(And trust my luck.)
The lowest branch was 10 feet up.
I had to jump and trust my luck.

7th Verse
And so I jumped
(And so I jumped)
Into the air
(Into the air)
And missed that branch,
(And missed that branch,)

A-way up there.
(A-way up there.)
And so I jumped into the air
And missed that branch, a-way up there.

8th Verse
Now don't you fret
(Now don't you fret)
And don't you frown.
(And don't you frown.)
I caught that branch
(I caught that branch)
On the way back down.
(On the way back down.)
Now don't you fret and don't you frown.
I caught that branch on the way back down.

9th Verse
That's all there is,
(That's all there is,)
There is no more,
(There is no more,)
Until I meet
(Until I meet)
That bear once more.
(That bear once more.)
That's all there is, there is no more,
Until I meet that bear once more.

10th Verse
The end, the end,
(The end, the end,)
The end, the end,
(The end, the end,)
The end, the end,
(The end, the end,)
The end, the end.
(The end, the end.)
The end, the end, the end, the end,
This time it really is the end!

Ravioli

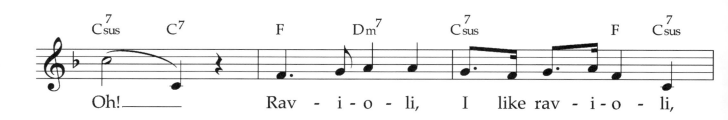

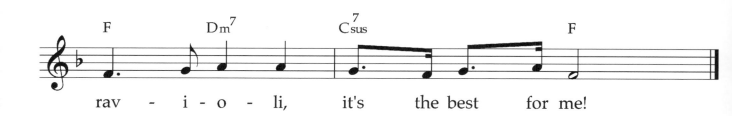

Ravioli (continued)

2nd Verse

Leader:	Do I have it in my hair?
Everyone:	Yes, you've got it in your hair!
Leader:	In my hair?
Everyone:	In your hair! Oh!

Everyone: Ravioli, I like ravioli,
                 Ravioli, it's the best for me!

3rd Verse

Leader:	Do I have it in my ears?
Everyone:	Yes, you've got in your ears!
Leader:	In my ears?
Everyone:	In your ears! Ew!

Everyone: Ravioli, I like ravioli,
                 Ravioli, it's the best for me!

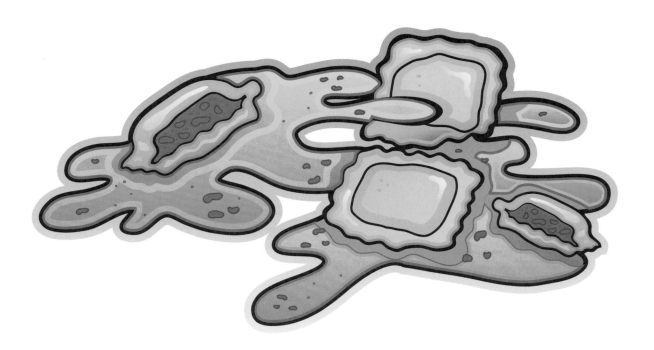

Little Bugs

There was a lit-tle mos-qui-to, and he was-n't an-y big-ger than the

head of a ver-y small pin, but the lump that he rais-es just

itch-es like the blaz-es and that's where the rub comes in. Comes—

in, comes— in, and— that's where the rub comes

in, oh, the lump that he rais-es just itch-es like the blaz-es and

that's where the rub comes in.

Little Bugs (continued)

2nd Verse
Said a thousand-legged worm, as he began to squirm,
"Has anybody seen a leg of mine?
If it can't be found I'll have to hop around
On the other nine hundred ninety-nine."

Hop around, hop around,
On the other nine hundred ninety-nine.
If it can't be found I'll have to hop around
On the other nine hundred ninety-nine.

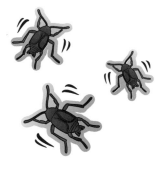

Read, Sing, and Play Along! Gross and Annoying Songs

Nobody Likes Me

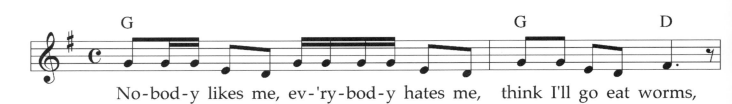

No-bod-y likes me, ev-'ry-bod-y hates me, think I'll go eat worms,

big   fat   juic - y   ones,   een - y   ween - y   squeem-y   ones,

see   how   they   wig - gle   and   squirm.

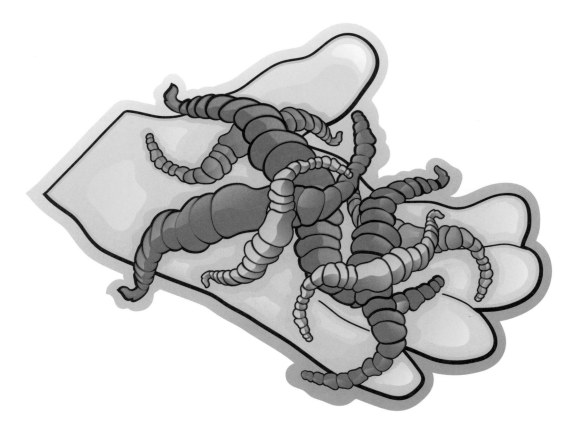

On Top of My Headache

On top of my head - ache _____ I had a sore throat. _____ My bones were all ach - ing, _____ I smelled like a goat. _____ My doc-tor pre - scribed _____ a trip on a boat _____ but a- las and a - lak dear _____ that boat will not

Read, Sing, and Play Along! Gross and Annoying Songs **241**

C

float._____ So now, I am writ -

ing_____ from un-der the sea._____

___ The joke's on my doc - tor._____ How

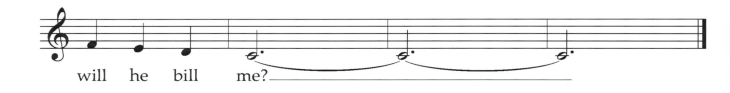

will he bill me?_____

Swing Low, Sweet Chariot

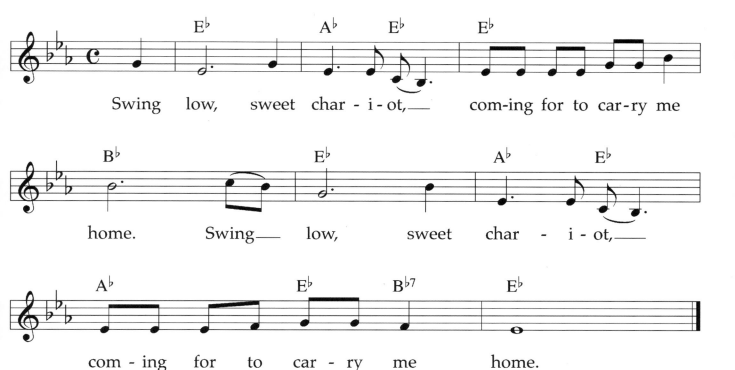

Swing low, sweet char - i - ot,— com-ing for to car-ry me home. Swing— low, sweet char - i - ot,— com - ing for to car - ry me home.

2nd Verse

I looked over Jordan and what
    did I see,
Coming for to carry me home.
A band of angels coming after me,
Coming for to carry me home.

Swing low, sweet chariot,
Coming for to carry me home.
Swing low, sweet chariot,
Coming for to carry me home.

3rd Verse

If you get there before I do,
Coming for to carry me home.
Tell all my friends I'm coming, too,
Coming for to carry me home.

Swing low, sweet chariot,
Coming for to carry me home.
Swing low, sweet chariot,
Coming for to carry me home.

Switch

I don't care if I go cra - zy, 1, 2, 3, 4, 5, 6, Switch!

Cra - zy go I, if care don't I, 6, 5, 4, 3, 2, 1, Switch!

It Ain't Gonna Rain No More

It ain't gon-na rain no more, no more, it ain't gon-na rain no more,

how in the heck can I wash my neck if it ain't gon-na rain no more?

Two Little Fleas

Shenandoah

Oh,   Shen - an-doah,_____   I long to   hear you,   a -

way,_____ you roll-ing   riv-er,_____   oh, Shen - an-doah,_____   I long to

hear you,_____   a - way,_____   I'm bound a - way,_____   'cross the

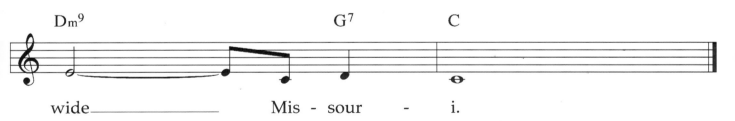

wide_____   Mis - sour - i.

2nd Verse
Oh, Shenandoah, I love your
    daughter,
Away, you rolling river,
I'll take her 'cross the rolling river,
Away, I'm bound away, 'cross the
    wide Missouri.

3rd Verse
Oh, Shenandoah, I long to hear you,
Away, you rolling river,
Oh, Shenandoah, I long to hear you,
Away, I'm bound away, 'cross the
    wide Missouri.

Have You Ever Seen

Have you ev - er seen a horse fly, a horse fly, a horse fly? Have you ev - er seen a horse fly? Now you tell us one.

2nd Verse
Have you ever seen a shoe box, a shoe box, a shoe box?
Have you ever seen a shoe box? Now you tell us one.

3rd Verse
Have you ever seen a chimney sweep, a chimney sweep, a chimney sweep?
Have you ever seen a chimney sweep? Now you tell us one.

4th Verse
Have you ever seen a dish mop, a dish mop, a dish mop?
Have you ever seen a dish mop? Now you tell us one.

I Went to Cincinnati

I— went to Cin-cin-nat-i and I walked a-round the block, and I

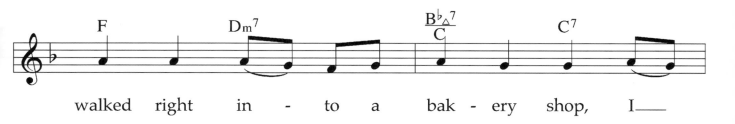

walked right in - to a bak-ery shop, I—

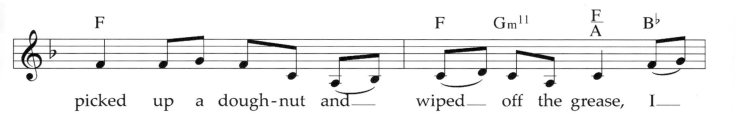

picked up a dough-nut and— wiped— off the grease, I—

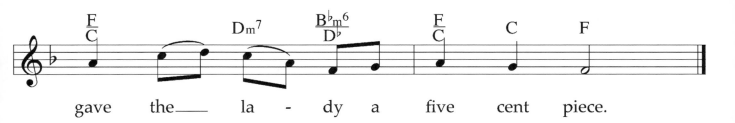

gave the— la - dy a five cent piece.

2nd Verse

Well, she looked at the nickel and she looked at me.
She said, "This nickel's no good to me.
There's a hole in the middle and it's all the way through."
Says I, "There's a hole in the doughnut, too!
Thanks for the doughnut, good-bye."

Read, Sing, and Play Along! Gross and Annoying Songs **249**

Chicken Sandwich

When I go in-to a rest-au-rant— this is what I cry, "Give—

me a chick-en sand-wich, cup of cof-fee, piece of pie!" And

these will be my fin-al words un - til the day I die, "Give

me a chick-en sand-wich, cup of cof-fee, piece of pie!"

Glo - ry, glo - ry,— what is it to you? Glo - ry, glo - ry,—

what is it to you? Glo - ry, glo - ry,— what is it to you, if I

have a chick-en sand-wich, cup of cof-fee, piece of pie?

Oh, My Monster, Frankenstein

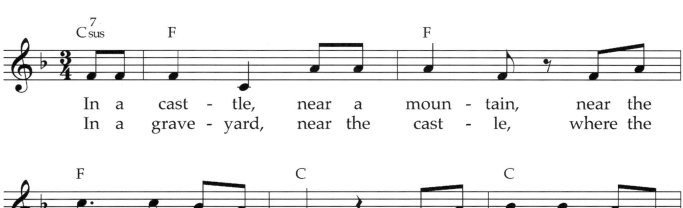

In a cast - tle, near a moun - tain, near the
In a grave - yard, near the cast - le, where the

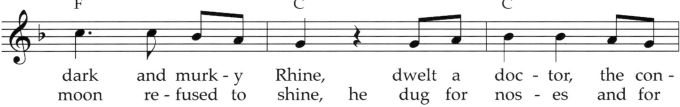

dark and murk - y Rhine, dwelt a doc - tor, the con -
moon re - fused to shine, he dug for nos - es and for

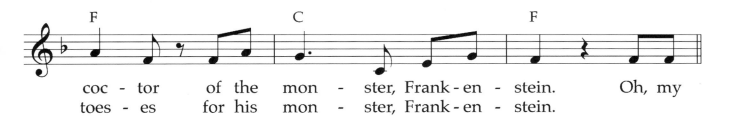

coc - tor of the mon - ster, Frank - en - stein. Oh, my
toes - es for his mon - ster, Frank - en - stein.

mon-ster, oh, my mon-ster, oh, my mon-ster, Frank-en-stein, you were

built to last for - ev - er, dread - ful scar - y, Frank - en - stein.

Read, Sing, and Play Along! Gross and Annoying Songs

Onward Christian Bedbugs

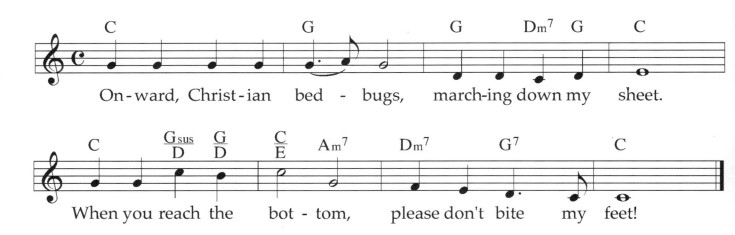

On-ward, Christ-ian bed - bugs, march-ing down my sheet.

When you reach the bot - tom, please don't bite my feet!

Take It Out, Remove It!

Oh, I stuck my head in a lit-tle skunk's hole, the lit-tle skunk said, "Up-on my soul, take it out, take it out, take it

1. out, re - move it!" Oh, I

2. out, re - move it!" Well, I

did-n't take it out and the lit-tle skunk said, "If you don't take it out you will wish that you were dead, take it out, take it out, PSSSSST! I re - moved it!

Miss Polly Had a Dolly

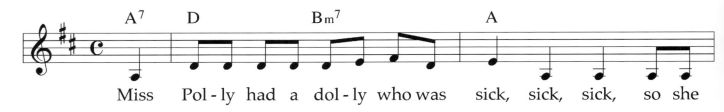

Miss Pol-ly had a dol-ly who was sick, sick, sick, so she

called for the doc-tor to come quick, quick, quick. The

doc-tor came with his bag and his hat, and he

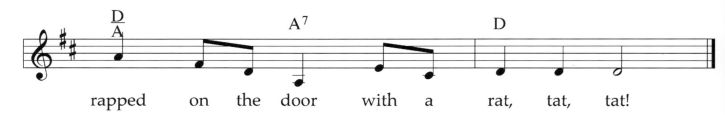

rapped on the door with a rat, tat, tat!

2nd Verse

He looked at the dolly and he shook his head,
And he said, "Miss Polly, put her straight to bed."
He wrote on the paper for a pill, pill, pill.
"I'll be back in the morning with the bill, bill, bill!"

Repeat all

The Ants Came Marching

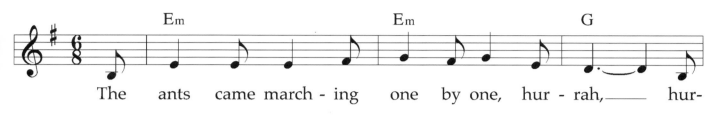

The ants came march - ing one by one, hur - rah,____ hur-

rah!____ The ants came march - ing one by one, hur - rah,____ hur-

rah!____ The ants came march - ing one by one, the

lit - tle one stopped to suck his thumb and they all go march ing

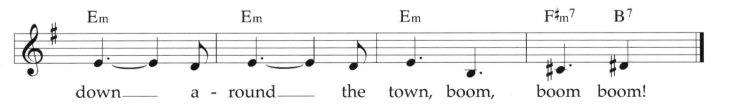

down____ a - round____ the town, boom, boom boom!

2nd Verse
The ants came marching two by two,
    hurrah, hurrah!
The ants came marching two by two,
    hurrah, hurrah!
The ants came marching two by two,
The little one stopped to tie his shoe
And they all go marching down around
    the town,
Boom, boom, boom!

3rd Verse
The ants came marching three by three,
    hurrah, hurrah!
The ants came marching three by three,
    hurrah, hurrah!
The ants came marching three by three,
The little one stopped to climb a tree
And they all go marching down around
    the town,
Boom, boom, boom!

Read, Sing, and Play Along! Gross and Annoying Songs

The Ants Came Marching (continued)

4th Verse

The ants came marching four by four,
    hurrah, hurrah!
The ants came marching four by four,
    hurrah, hurrah!
The ants came marching four by four,
The little one stopped to shut the door
And they all go marching down around
    the town,
Boom, boom, boom!

5th Verse

The ants came marching five by five,
    hurrah, hurrah!
The ants came marching five by five,
    hurrah, hurrah!
The ants came marching five by five,
The little one stopped to take a dive
And they all go marching down around
    the town,
Boom, boom, boom!

6th Verse

The ants came marching six by six,
    hurrah, hurrah!
The ants came marching six by six,
    hurrah, hurrah!
The ants came marching six by six,
The little one stopped to pick up sticks
And they all go marching down around
    the town,
Boom, boom, boom!

7th Verse

The ants came marching seven by seven,
    hurrah, hurrah!
The ants came marching seven by seven,
    hurrah, hurrah!
The ants came marching seven by seven,
The little one stopped to go to heaven
And they all go marching down around
    the town,
Boom, boom, boom!

8th Verse

The ants came marching eight by eight,
    hurrah, hurrah!
The ants came marching eight by eight,
    hurrah, hurrah!
The ants came marching eight by eight,
The little one stopped to shut the gate
And they all go marching down around
    the town,
Boom, boom, boom!

9th Verse

The ants came marching nine by nine,
    hurrah, hurrah!
The ants came marching nine by nine,
    hurrah, hurrah!
The ants came marching nine by nine,
The little one stopped to scratch his spine
And they all go marching down around
    the town,
Boom, boom, boom!

10th Verse

The ants came marching ten by ten,
    hurrah, hurrah!
The ants came marching ten by ten,
    hurrah, hurrah!
The ants came marching ten by ten,
The little one stopped to say, "THE END,"
And they all go marching down around
    the town.

The Green Grass Grew All Around

Oh, in the woods there was a tree, the

pret-ti-est lit-tle tree that you ev-er did see. And the

tree was in the ground, and the green grass grew all a-

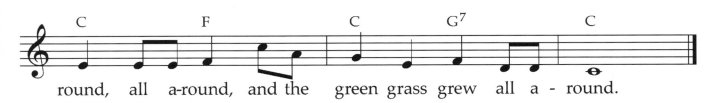

round, all a-round, and the green grass grew all a-round.

Read, Sing, and Play Along! Gross and Annoying Songs **257**

The Green Grass Grew All Around (continued)

2nd Verse
And on this tree there was a limb,
The prettiest little limb that you ever did see.
And the tree was in the ground,
And the green grass grew all around, all around,
And the green grass grew all around.

3rd Verse
And on this limb there was a branch,
The prettiest little branch that you ever did see.
And the branch was on the tree,
And the tree was in the ground,
And the green grass grew all around, all around,
And the green grass grew all around.

4th Verse
And on this branch there was a twig,
The prettiest little twig that you ever did see.
And the twig was on the branch,
And the branch was on the tree,
And the tree was in the ground,
And the green grass grew all around, all around,
And the green grass grew all around.

5th Verse
And on this twig there was a leaf,
The prettiest little leaf that you ever did see.
And the leaf was on the twig,
And the twig was on the branch,
And the branch was on the tree,
And the tree was in the ground,
And the green grass grew all around, all around,
And the green grass grew all around.

Down by the Bay

Read, Sing, and Play Along! Gross and Annoying Songs

Down by the Bay (continued)

2nd Verse
Down by the bay
(Down by the bay)
Where the watermelons grow,
(Where the watermelons grow,)
Back to my home
(Back to my home)
I dare not go.
(I dare not go.)
For if I do
(For if I do)
My mother will say,
(My mother will say,)
"Did you ever see a frog walking his
      dog?" Down by the bay!

3rd Verse
Down by the bay
(Down by the bay)
Where the watermelons grow,
(Where the watermelons grow,)
Back to my home
(Back to my home)
I dare not go.
(I dare not go.)
For if I do
(For if I do)
My mother will say,
(My mother will say,)
"Did you ever see a fly wearing a
      tie?" Down by the bay!

4th Verse
Down by the bay
(Down by the bay)
Where the watermelons grow,
(Where the watermelons grow,)
Back to my home
(Back to my home)
I dare not go.
(I dare not go.)
For if I do
(For if I do)
My mother will say,
(My mother will say,)
"Did you ever see a bear combing
      his hair?" Down by the bay!

Peace Like a River

The Bear Went Over the Mountain

The bear went o-ver the moun-tain, the bear went o-ver the

moun-tain, the bear went o-ver the moun-tain to

see what he could see.___ To see what he could see,___ to

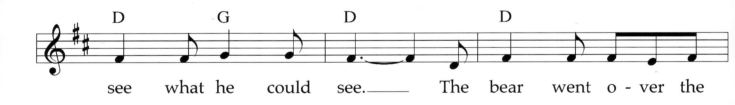

see what he could see.___ The bear went o-ver the

moun-tain, the bear went o-ver the moun-tain, the

bear went o-ver the moun-tain to see what he could see.

The Bear Went Over the Mountain (continued)

2nd Verse
The other side of the mountain,
The other side of the mountain,
The other side of the mountain
Was all that he could see.

Was all that he could see,
Was all that he could see.

The other side of the mountain,
The other side of the mountain,
The other side of the mountain
Was all that he could see.

She'll Be Comin' 'Round the Mountain

She'll be com-in' 'round the moun-tain when she comes. She'll be

com-in' 'round the moun-tain when she comes. She'll be

com-in' 'round the moun-tain, she'll be com-in' 'round the moun-tain, she'll be

com-in' 'round the moun-tain when she comes.

She'll Be Comin' 'Round the Mountain (continued)

2nd Verse
She'll be driving six white horses when she comes.
She'll be driving six white horses when she comes.
She'll be driving six white horses,
She'll be driving six white horses,
She'll be driving six white horses when she comes.

3rd Verse
She will wear red pajamas when she comes.
She will wear red pajamas when she comes.
She will wear red pajamas,
She will wear red pajamas,
She will wear red pajamas when she comes.

4th Verse
She will have to sleep with Grandma when she comes.
She will have to sleep with Grandma when she comes.
She will have to sleep with Grandma,
She will have to sleep with Grandma,
She will have to sleep with Grandma when she comes.

Itsy Bitsy's Birthday

The its-y bits-y spid-er climbed up the birth-day cake.

Its-y bit-sy quick-ly learned he'd made a big mis-take. He

climbed up on the can-dle be-fore the cake was cut, _____ the

its-y bits-y spid-er, he burned his lit-tle butt!

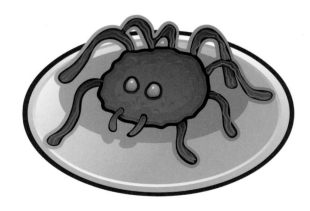

Announcements

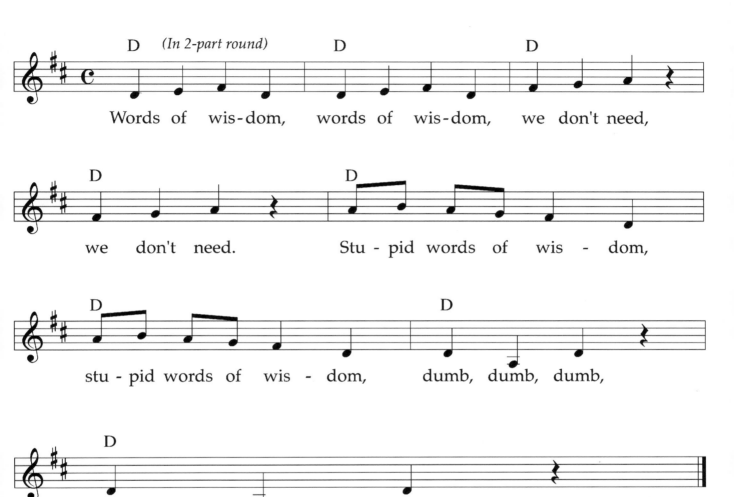

Words of wis-dom, words of wis-dom, we don't need,

we don't need. Stu - pid words of wis - dom,

stu - pid words of wis - dom, dumb, dumb, dumb,

dumb, dumb, dumb!

Sweet Betsy From Pike

Did you ev-er hear of sweet Bet-sy from Pike who

crossed the wide prair-ie with her hus-band Ike, with

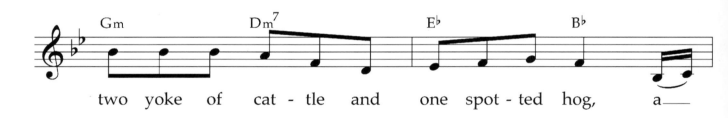

two yoke of cat-tle and one spot-ted hog, a——

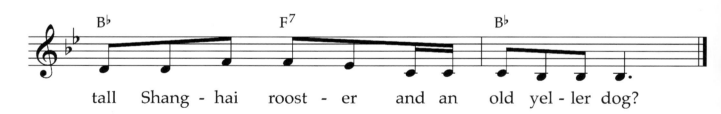

tall Shang-hai roost-er and an old yel-ler dog?

Sing toorali, oorali, oorali aye
Sing toorali, oorali, oorali aye
Sing toorali, oorali, oorali aye
Sing toorali, oorali, oorali aye

Sweet Betsy From Pike (continued)

2nd Verse
The alkali desert was burning and bare
And Ike cried in fear, "We are lost, I declare!
My dear old Pike County, I'll go back to you."
Said Betsy, "You'll go by yourself, if you do."

Sing toorali, oorali, oorali aye
Sing toorali, oorali, oorali aye
Sing toorali, oorali, oorali aye
Sing toorali, oorali, oorali aye

3rd Verse
They swam the wide rivers and crossed the tall peaks.
They camped on the prairie for weeks upon weeks.
They fought off the Indians with musket and ball
And reached California in spite of it all.

Sing toorali, oorali, oorali aye
Sing toorali, oorali, oorali aye
Sing toorali, oorali, oorali aye
Sing toorali, oorali, oorali aye

Johnny Had a Head
Like a Ping-Pong Ball

John - ny had a head like a ping - pong ball,

John - ny had a head like a ping - pong ball,

John-ny had a head like a ping - pong ball, ping - pong ball!_____

Ping-pong, ping-pong, ping-pong, ping-pong, ping-pong, ping-pong, ping-pong ball!

Ping-pong, ping-pong, ping-pong, ping-pong, ping-pong, ping-pong, ping-pong ball!

Ping-pong, ping-pong, ping-pong, ping-pong, ping-pong, ping-pong, ping-pong ball!

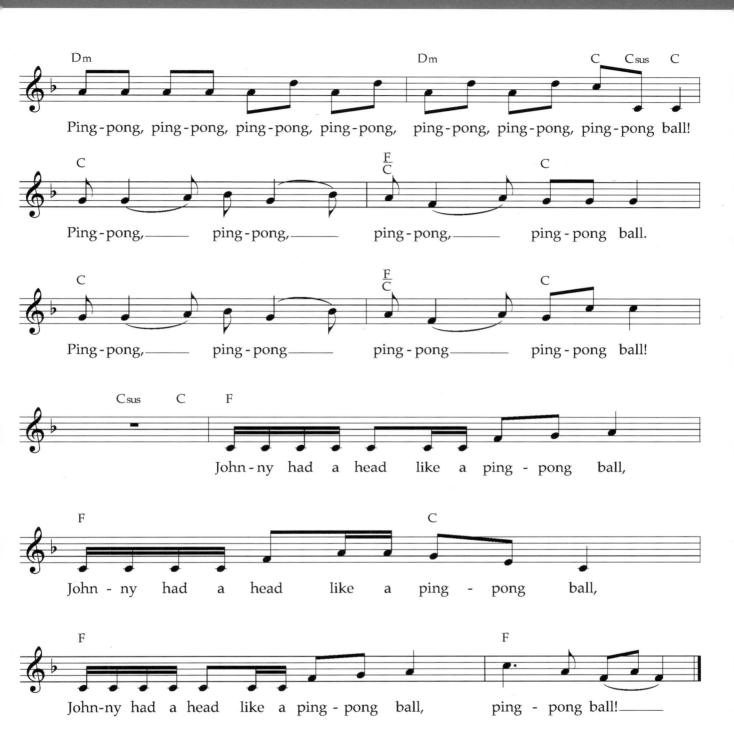

Repeat from measure five

The Littlest Worm

The lit-tlest worm *The lit-tlest worm* I ev er

saw, *I ev-er saw,* was stuck in - side *was stuck in-side* my so-da

straw. *my so-da straw.* The lit-tlest worm *the lit-tlest worm* I ev er

saw, *I ev-er saw,* was stuck in - side *was stuck in-side* my so-da

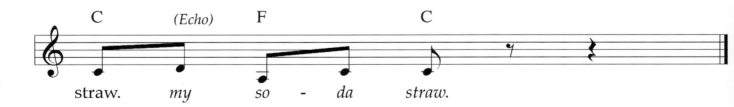

straw. *my so - da straw.*

2nd Verse

He said to me,
(He said to me,)
"Don't take a sip.
("Don't take a sip.)
For if you do,
(For if you do,)
I'll surely flip!"
(I'll surely flip!")
He said to me,
(He said to me,)
"Don't take a sip.
("Don't take a sip.)
For if you do,
(For if you do,)
I'll surely flip!"
(I'll surely flip!")

3rd Verse

I took a sip
(I took a sip)
And he went down,
(And he went down,)
All through my pipes,
(All through my pipes,)
He surely drowned.
(He surely drowned.)
I took a sip
(I took a sip)
And he went down,
(And he went down,)
All through my pipes,
(All through my pipes,)
He surely drowned.
(He surely drowned.)

4th Verse

He was my pal,
(He was my pal,)
He was my friend,
(He was my friend,)
But now he's gone
(But now he's gone)
And that's the end.
(And that's the end.)
He was my pal,
(He was my pal,)
He was my friend,
(He was my friend,)
But now he's gone
(But now he's gone)
And that's the end.
(And that's the end.)

5th Verse

The moral of
(The moral of)
This story is
(This story is)
Don't take a sip
(Don't take a sip)
Of soda fizz.
(Of soda fizz.)
The moral of
(The moral of)
This story is
(This story is)
Don't take a sip
(Don't take a sip)
Of soda fizz.
(Of soda fizz.)

The Cat Came Back

2nd Verse
Well, they gave a boy a dollar for to
  set the cat afloat,
And he took him up the river in a
  sack and a boat.
Now the fishing, it was fine 'til the
  news got around
That the boat was missing and the
  boy was drowned.

Chorus:
**But the cat came back the very
  next day,**
They thought he was a goner
But the cat came back
'Cause he wouldn't stay away.

3rd Verse
Well, the farmer on the corner said
  he'd shoot him on sight,
And he loaded up his gun full of
  rocks and dynamite.
The gun went off, heard all over
  town,
Little pieces of the man was all that
  they found.

Chorus

3rd Verse
Now, they gave him to a man going
  up in a balloon,
And they told him for to leave him
  with the man in the moon.
The balloon it busted, back to earth
  did head,
Seven miles away they picked the
  man up dead.

Chorus

4th Verse
Well, they finally found a way for
  this cat for to fix,
They put him in an orange crate on
  Route 66.
Come a ten-ton truck with a 20-ton
  load,
Scattered pieces of the orange crate
  all down the road.

Chorus

5th Verse
Well, they took him to the shop
  where the meat was ground,
And they dropped him in the hopper
  when the butcher wasn't 'round.
Well, the cat disappeared with a
  blood-curdling shriek,
And the town's meat tasted furry for
  a week.

Chorus

6th Verse
And from Cape Canaveral they put
  him into place,
Shot him in a rocket going way out
  in space.
And they finally thought the cat
  was out of human reach,
Next day they got a call from
  Miami Beach.

Chorus

Yuck! Cats!

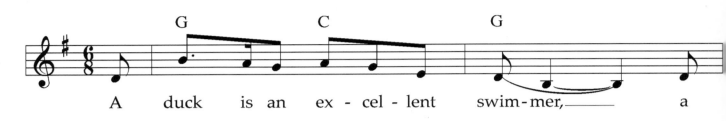

A duck is an ex-cel-lent swim-mer,_____ a

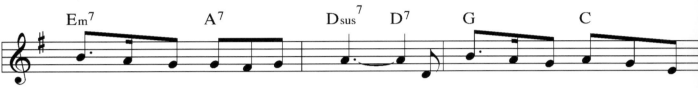

mon-key's both clev-er and shrewd,_____ a dog loves to bring you your

slip-pers,_____ but cats on-ly come when there's food.

Yuck! Cats! Yuck! Cats! Don't try to give one to me._____

Yuck! Cats! Yuck! Cats! Don't try to give one to me.

Yuck! Cats! (continued)

2nd Verse
Birds chirp and twitter for hours,
Rabbits make cuddly pets,
Snakes can even be playful,
But cats like to play hard to get!

Chorus:
Yuck! Cats! Yuck! Cats!
Don't try to give one to me.
Yuck! Cats! Yuck! Cats!
Don't try to give on to me.

3rd Verse
Donkeys are known to be stubborn,
But cats are much worse, you'll agree,
Try leading a cat to the water,
It's easier to part the Red Sea!

Chorus

4th Verse
Cat lovers say cats are so loving,
So diligent, loyal, and true,
But cats just know how to be sneaky,
Ignore folks, chase mice, and go "Mew!"

Chorus

Elbows off the Table

Su-sie, Su-sie, if you're a-ble, get your el-bows off the ta-ble,

this is not a hors-e's sta-ble, but a res-pec-ta-ble din-ing ta-ble.

2nd Verse
Michael, Michael, if you're able,
Get your elbows off the table,
This is not a horse's stable,
But a respectable dining table.

Repeat all

I Had a Cat

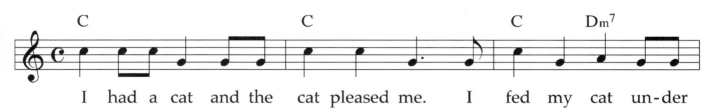

I had a cat and the cat pleased me. I fed my cat un-der

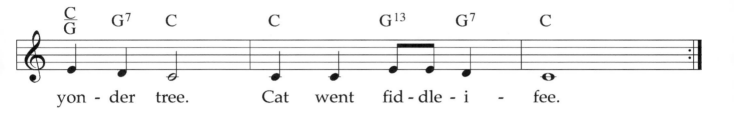

yon-der tree. Cat went fid-dle-i-fee.

2nd Verse
I had a dog and the dog pleased me.
I fed my dog under yonder tree.
Dog went bow-wow, bow-wow.
Cat went fiddle-i-fee.

3rd Verse
I had a hen and the hen pleased me.
I fed my hen under yonder tree.
Hen went ka-ka, ka-ka.
Dog went bow-wow, bow-wow.
Cat went fiddle-i-fee.

4th Verse
I had a duck and the duck pleased me.
I fed my duck under yonder tree.
Duck went quack-quack, quack-quack.
Hen went ka-ka, ka-ka.
Dog went bow-wow, bow-wow.
Cat went fiddle-i-fee.

5th Verse
I had a sheep and the sheep pleased me.
I fed my sheep under yonder tree.
Sheep went baa-baa, baa-baa.
Duck went quack-quack, quack-quack.
Hen went ka-ka, ka-ka.
Dog went bow-wow, bow-wow.
Cat went fiddle-i-fee.

Do Your Ears Hang Low?

Do your   ears hang low? Do they wob-ble to and fro? Can you

tie them in   a knot?   Can you   tie them in   a bow?   Can you

throw them o'er your shoul-der like a Con-tin-en-tal sol-dier? Do your

ears   hang_____ low?

Do Your Ears Hang Low? (continued)

2nd Verse

Do your ears hang high? Do they reach up to the sky?
Do they wrinkle when they're wet? Do they straighten when they're dry?
Can you wave 'em at your neighbor with an element of flavor?
Do your ears hang high?

3rd Verse

Do your ears hang wide? Do they flap from side to side?
Do they wave in the breeze from the slightest little sneeze?
Can you soar above the nation with a feeling of elevation?
Do your ears hang wide?

4th Verse

Do your ears fall off when you give a great big cough?
Do they lie there on the ground or bounce up at every sound?
Can you stick 'em in your pocket just like Davy Crocket?
Do your ears fall off?

Read, Sing, and Play Along! Gross and Annoying Songs

A Sailor Went to Sea

A sail-or went to sea, sea, sea, to see what he could see, see, see, but

all that he could see, see, see, was the bot-tom of the deep blue sea, sea, sea!

Oh, Tom the Toad

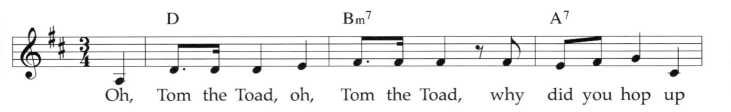

Oh, Tom the Toad, oh, Tom the Toad, why did you hop up

on the road? Oh, Tom the Toad, oh, Tom the Toad, why

did you hop up on the road? You were my friend, and

now you're dead, you bear the marks of tire tread. Oh,

Tom the Toad, oh, Tom the Toad, why did you hop up on the road?

Oh, Tom the Toad (continued)

2nd Verse
Oh, Tom the Toad,
Oh, Tom the Toad
Why did you hop up on the road?
Oh, Tom the Toad,
Oh, Tom the Toad
Why did you hop up on the road?
You did not see yon passing car,
And now you're stretched out on the tar.
Oh, Tom the Toad,
Oh, Tom the Toad
Why did you hop up on the road?

Greeting Song

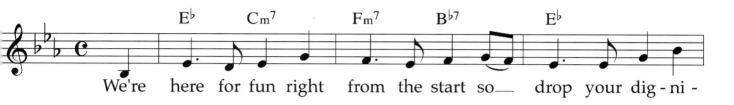

We're here for fun right from the start so— drop your dig - ni -

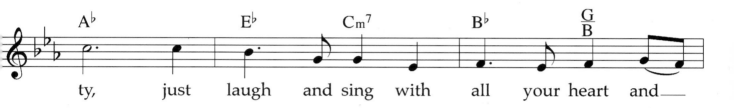

ty, just laugh and sing with all your heart and—

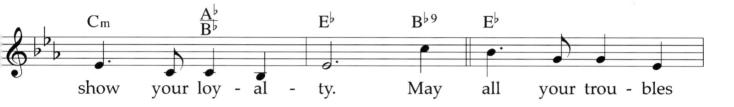

show your loy - al - ty. May all your trou - bles

be for-got, let this night be the best. Join

in the songs we sing to-night, be— hap-py with the rest.

Row, Row, Row Your Boat

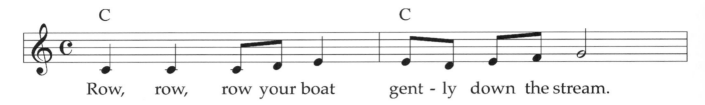

Row, row, row your boat gent - ly down the stream.

Merr-'ly, Merr-'ly, Merr-'ly, Merr-'ly, life is but a dream.

Repeat 2X in 2-part round

Home on the Range

A Peanut Sat on a Railroad Track

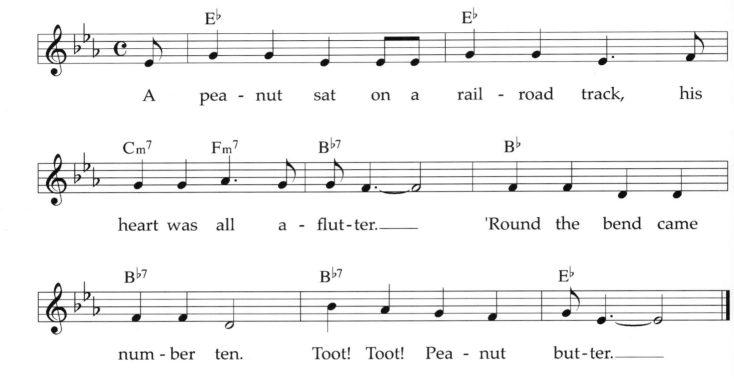

A pea - nut sat on a rail - road track, his

heart was all a - flut - ter.—— 'Round the bend came

num - ber ten. Toot! Toot! Pea - nut but - ter.——

2nd Verse
A peanut sat on a railroad track,
His heart was all a-flutter.
'Round the bend came number ten.
Toot! Toot! Peanut butter.

3rd Verse
A peanut sat on a railroad track,
His heart was all a-flutter.
'Round the bend came number ten.
Toot! Toot! Peanut butter.

SQUISH!

Bug Juice

At the   camp with the   boy   scouts,_____   they
frui -   ty_____   liked

gave us a   drink._____   We____ thought it was
tast - y Kool - aid,_____   but the bugs that were

Kool -   aid,_____   be - cause it was pink._____
in   it,_____   were mur - dered with Raid._____

_____   But the   thing that they told   us,_____
_____   We drank it by the gal - lons_____

____ would - 've grossed out a moose,_____   for that
____ we drank it by the tons,_____

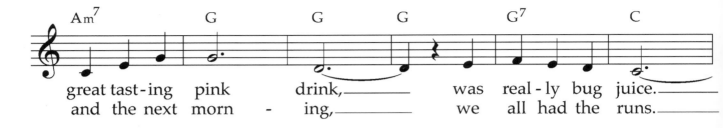

great tast-ing   pink   drink,_____   was   real-ly   bug   juice._____
and   the   next   morn   -   ing,_____   we   all   had   the   runs._____

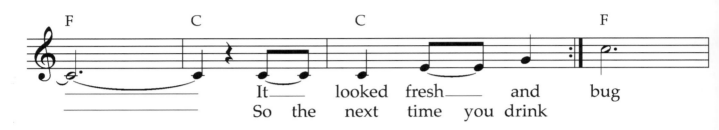

_____   It_____   looked   fresh_____   and   bug
So   the   next   time   you   drink

juice,_____   and   a   fly   drives   you   mad,_____

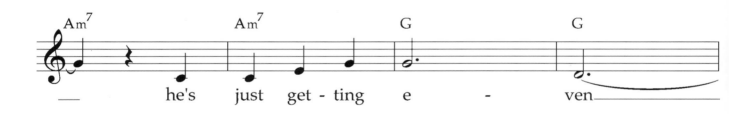

_____   he's   just   get - ting   e   -   ven_____

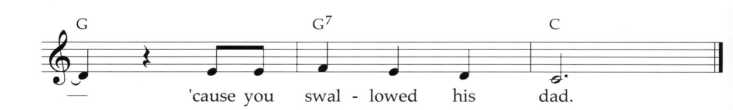

_____   'cause   you   swal - lowed   his   dad.

Animal Fair

Read, Sing, and Play Along! Gross and Annoying Songs

Animal Fair (continued)

2nd Verse
I went to the animal fair.
The birds and the beasts were there.
The big baboon by the light of the moon,
Was combing his auburn hair.
You ought to have seen the monk.
He jumped on the elephant's trunk.
The elephant sneezed and fell on his knees,
And what became of the monk,
The monk, the monk, the monk,
The monk, the monk, the monk.
The monk, the monk, the monk!

Monkey See, Monkey Do

The mon-key stamp, stamp, stamps his feet,____ the mon-key

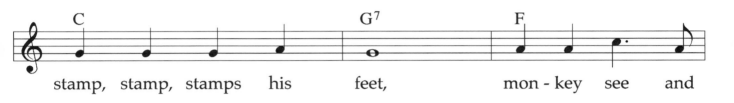

stamp, stamp, stamps his feet, mon-key see and

mon-key do, the mon-key does the same as you!

2nd Verse
The monkey clap, clap, claps his hands,
The monkey clap, clap, claps his hands,
Monkey see and monkey do,
The monkey does the same as you!

3rd Verse
When you make a funny face,
The monkey makes a funny face,
Monkey see and monkey do,
The monkey does the same as you!

My Name Is Yon Yonson

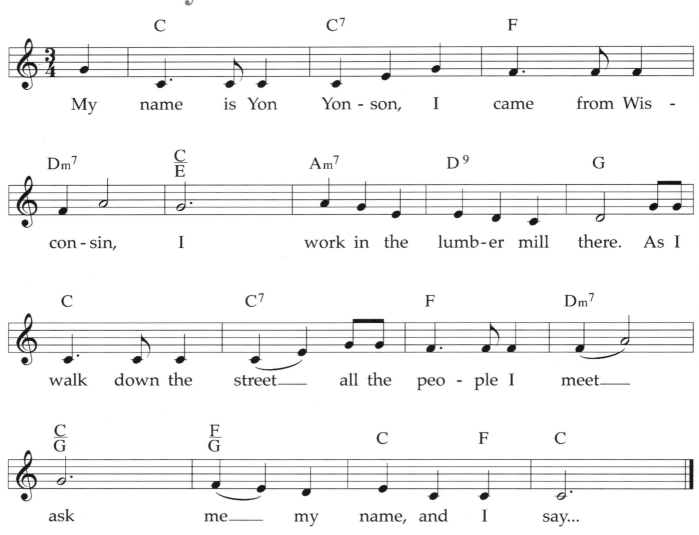

My name is Yon Yon-son, I came from Wis-con-sin, I work in the lumb-er mill there. As I walk down the street____ all the peo-ple I meet____ ask me____ my name, and I say...

There's a Hole in the Bucket

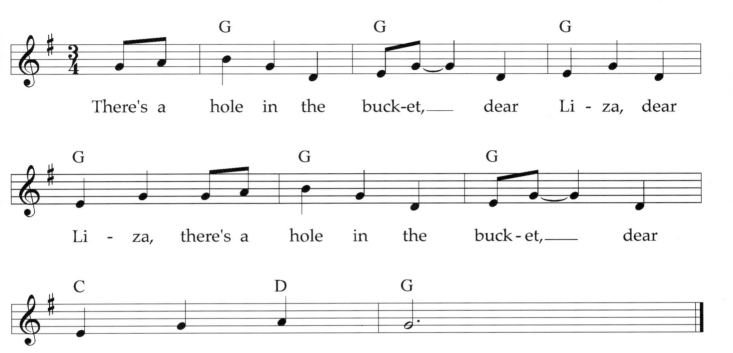

There's a hole in the buck-et,— dear Li - za, dear

Li - za, there's a hole in the buck-et,— dear

Li - za a hole!

2nd Verse
Then fix it, dear Henry,
Dear Henry, dear Henry,
Then fix it, dear Henry,
Dear Henry, fix it!

3rd Verse
With what shall I fix it,
Dear Liza, dear Liza?
With what shall I fix it,
Dear Liza, with what?

4th Verse
With a straw, dear Henry,
Dear Henry, dear Henry,
With a straw, dear Henry,
Dear Henry, a straw!

5th Verse
But the straw is too long,
Dear Liza, dear Liza,
But the straw is too long,
Dear Liza, too long.

6th Verse
Then cut it, dear Henry,
Dear Henry, dear Henry,
Then cut it, dear Henry,
Dear Henry, cut it!

7th Verse
With what shall I cut it,
Dear Liza, dear Liza?
With what shall I cut it,
Dear Liza, with what?

Read, Sing, and Play Along! Gross and Annoying Songs 295

There's a Hole in the Bucket (continued)

8th Verse
With an axe, dear Henry,
Dear Henry, dear Henry,
With an axe, dear Henry,
Dear Henry, an axe!

9th Verse
The axe is too dull,
Dear Liza, dear Liza,
The axe is too dull,
Dear Liza, too dull.

10th Verse
Then sharpen it, dear Henry,
Dear Henry, dear Henry,
Then sharpen it, dear Henry,
Dear Henry, sharpen it!

11th Verse
With what shall I sharpen it,
Dear Liza, dear Liza?
With what shall I sharpen it,
Dear Liza, with what?

12th Verse
With a stone, dear Henry,
Dear Henry, dear Henry,
With a stone, dear Henry,
Dear Henry, a stone!

13th Verse
The stone is too dry,
Dear Liza, dear Liza,
The stone is too dry,
Dear Liza, too dry.

14th Verse
Then wet it, dear Henry,
Dear Henry, dear Henry,
Then wet it, dear Henry,
Dear Henry, wet it!

15th Verse
With what shall I wet it,
Dear Liza, dear Liza?
With what shall I wet it,
Dear Liza, with what?

16th Verse
With water, dear Henry,
Dear Henry, dear Henry,
With water, dear Henry,
Dear Henry, water!

17th Verse
How shall I get it,
Dear Liza, dear Liza?
How shall I get it,
Dear Liza, get it?

18th Verse
In the bucket, dear Henry,
Dear Henry, dear Henry,
In the bucket, dear Henry,
Dear Henry, the bucket!

19th Verse
There's a hole in the bucket,
Dear Liza, dear Liza,
There's a hole in the bucket,
Dear Liza, a hole.

20th Verse
Then fix it, dear Henry,
Dear Henry, dear Henry,
Then fix it, dear Henry,
Dear Henry, fix it!

The Preposition Song

With on for af-ter at by in a - gainst in-stead of near be-tween,

through o-ver up ac-cord-ing to a - round a-mong be-yond in-to,

un-til with - in with-out up - on from a - bove a - cross a - long,

toward be-fore be-hind be - low be - neath be-side dur-ing un-der.

Rueben and Rachel

Rue-ben, Rue-ben, I've been think-ing what a fine world this would be

if the men were all trans-port-ed   far be-yond the North-ern Sea!

2nd Verse
Oh, my goodness gracious, Rachel, what a strange world this would be
If the men were all transported far beyond the Northern Sea!

3rd Verse
Reuben, Reuben, I've been thinking what a great life girls would lead
If they had no men about them, none to tease them, none to heed!

4th Verse
Rachel, Rachel, I've been thinking life would be so easy then,
What a lovely world this would be if you'd leave it to the men!

I Eat My Peas With Honey

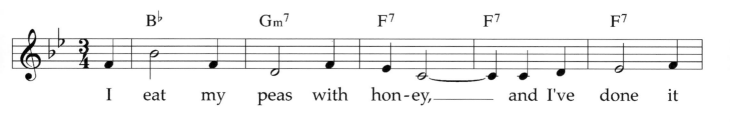

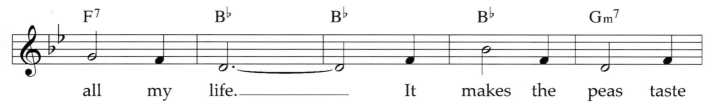

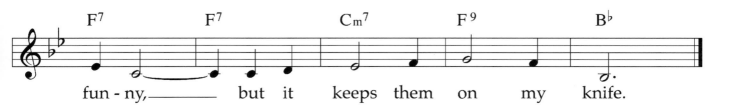

Read, Sing, and Play Along! Gross and Annoying Songs

The More We Get Together

The— more we get to - geth - er, to - geth - er, to - geth - er, the— more we get to - geth - er the hap-pi - er we'll be. For your friends are my friends and my friends are your friends. The— more we get to - geth - er the hap-pi - er we'll be.

S-M-I-L-E

It is - n't an - y trou - ble just to S - M - I - L - E. It

is - n't an - y trou - ble just to S - M - I - L - E. It

is - n't an - y trou - ble just to S - M - I - L - E, to S - M - I - L -

E. So smile when you are in trou - ble.

It will van - ish like a bub - ble, if you'll on - ly take the

trou - ble to S - M - I - L - E!

Read, Sing, and Play Along! Gross and Annoying Songs **301**

No L

Oh, Susanna!

The Baby Bumblebee

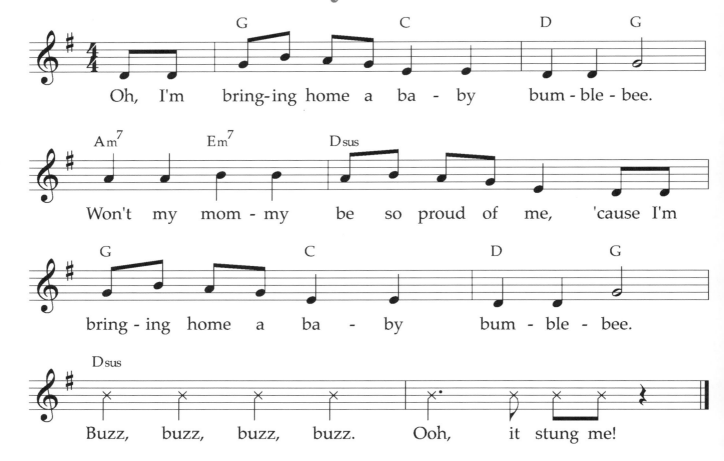

Oh, I'm bring-ing home a ba - by bum - ble - bee.

Won't my mom - my be so proud of me, 'cause I'm

bring - ing home a ba - by bum - ble - bee.

Buzz, buzz, buzz, buzz. Ooh, it stung me!

2nd Verse

Oh, I'm bringing home a baby rattlesnake.
Won't my mommy shiver and shake,
'Cause I'm bringing home a baby rattlesnake.
(Spoken):   *Rattle, rattle, rattle.*
        Ooh, it bit me!

3rd Verse

Oh, I'm bringing home a baby dinosaur.
Won't my mommy fall right through the floor,
'Cause I'm bringing home a baby dinosaur.
(Spoken):   *Gobble, gobble, gobble.*
        Ooh, it ate me!

Father Abraham

Fath - er   A - bra-ham—— had man - y   sons,   man - y

sons had Fath - er   A - bra-ham,   I am   one   of them—— and so are

you,   so   let's   just   praise   the   Lord, Right   arm!

2nd Verse
Father Abraham had many sons,
Many sons had Father Abraham,
I am one of them, and so are you,
So let's just praise the Lord,
Right arm! Left arm!

3rd Verse
Father Abraham had many sons,
Many sons had Father Abraham,
I am one of them, and so are you,
So let's just praise the Lord,
Right arm! Left arm! Right foot!

Father Abraham (continued)

4th Verse
Father Abraham had many sons,
Many sons had Father Abraham,
I am one of them, and so are you,
So let's just praise the Lord,
Right arm! Left arm! Right foot! Left foot!

5th Verse
Father Abraham had many sons,
Many sons had Father Abraham,
I am one of them, and so are you,
So let's just praise the Lord,
Right arm! Left arm! Right foot! Left foot!
Chin up!

6th Verse
Father Abraham had many sons,
Many sons had Father Abraham,
I am one of them, and so are you,
So let's just praise the Lord,
Right arm! Left arm! Right foot! Left foot!
Chin up! Turn around!

7th Verse
Father Abraham had many sons,
Many sons had Father Abraham,
I am one of them, and so are you,
So let's just praise the Lord,
Right arm! Left arm! Right foot! Left foot!
Chin up! Turn around! Sit down!

Roadkill Stew

Road - kill   stew!   Road - kill   stew!

*May be sung as a round beginning here.

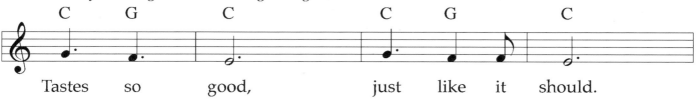

Tastes   so   good,   just   like   it   should.

First you go down to the   in - ter-state, you   wait for the crit - ter to

meet   its fate. You   take   it home and you   make   it great!

Road - kill   stew!   Road - kill   stew!

Bring Back My Neighbors to Me

Last night as I lay on my pil-low,_____ last

night as I lay on my bed,_____ I stuck__ my feet out the

win-dow,_____ in the morn-ing my neigh-bors were dead.

Bring back, bring back, bring back my neigh-bors to me._____

Bring back, bring back, bring back my neigh-bors to me.

Biblical Baseball Game

Eve stold first and Ad-am sec-ond, Saint Pe-ter um-pired the

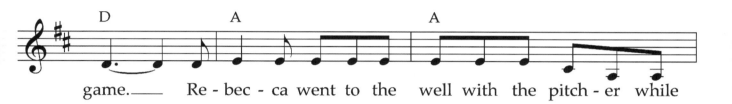

game.—— Re - bec - ca went to the well with the pitch - er while

Ruth, in the field, won fame!—— Go - li -ath was struck out by

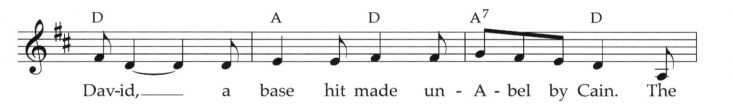

Dav-id,—— a base hit made un - A - bel by Cain. The

prod - i - gal son made— one home run, broth-er

No - ah gave out checks for the rain.

Michael Finnegan

There once was a man name Mi - chael Fin - ne - gan.

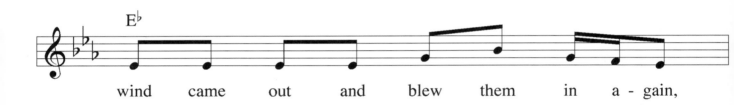

He grew whisk - ers on his chin - ne - gan. The

wind came out and blew them in a - gain,

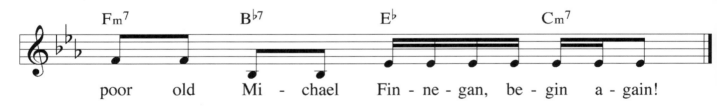

poor old Mi - chael Fin - ne - gan, be - gin a - gain!

2nd Verse
There once was a man named
    Michael Finnegan.
He went fishing with a pinnegan.
Caught a fish but he dropped
    it in again,
Poor old Michael Finnegan,
    begin again!

3rd Verse
There once was a man named
    Michael Finnegan.
Climbed a tree and barked
    his shinnigan.

Took offer several yards
    of skinnigan,
Poor old Michael Finnegan,
    begin again!

4th Verse
There once was a man named
    Michael Finnegan.
He grew fat and he grew thin again.
Then he died and we have to
    begin again,
Poor old Michael Finnegan,
    begin again!

Oh, My Darling, Clementine

In a cav - ern, in a can - yon, ex - ca - va - ting for a

mine, dwelt a min - er for - ty nin - er and his

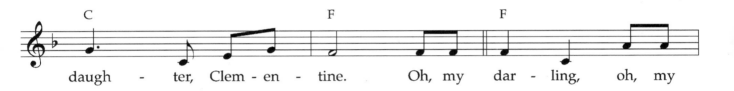

daugh - ter, Clem - en - tine. Oh, my dar - ling, oh, my

dar - ling, oh, my dar - ling, Clem - en - tine, you are

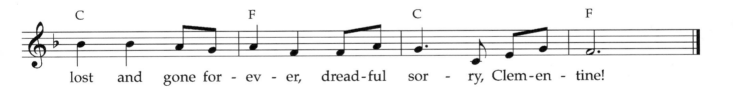

lost and gone for - ev - er, dread - ful sor - ry, Clem - en - tine!

Oh, My Darling, Clementine (continued)

2nd Verse
Drove her ducklings to the water every morning just at nine,
Hit her foot against a splinter fell into the foaming brine.

3rd Verse
Ruby lips above the water, blowing bubbles soft and fine,
But alas, I was no swimmer so I lost my Clementine!

4th Verse
Now you scouts may learn the moral of this little tale of mine,
Artificial respiration would have saved my Clementine!

5th Verse
How I missed her, how I missed her, how I missed my Clementine,
'Til I kissed her little sister and forgot my Clementine!

Nero, My Dog, Has Fleas

The Baby Prune

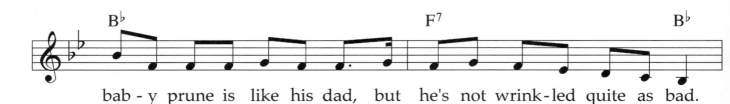

No mat-ter how young a prune may be, he's al-ways full of wrink-les. A

bab-y prune is like his dad, but he's not wrink-led quite as bad.

We have wrink-les on our face, *a prune has wrink-les ev-'ry place!* No

mat-ter how young a prune may be, he's al-ways full of wrink-les.

(Spoken)

Same song, sec-ond verse, a lit-tle bit loud-er and a lit-tle bit worse!

Same song, third verse, a little bit louder and a little bit worse!

How Much Wood

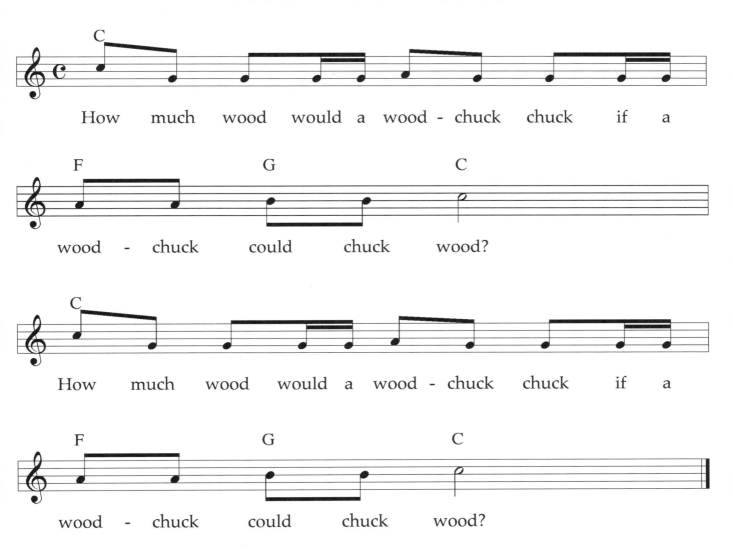

How much wood would a wood - chuck chuck if a

wood - chuck could chuck wood?

How much wood would a wood - chuck chuck if a

wood - chuck could chuck wood?

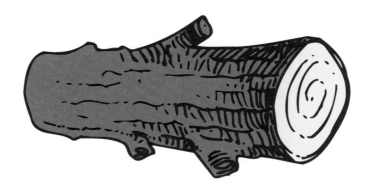

Sally the Camel

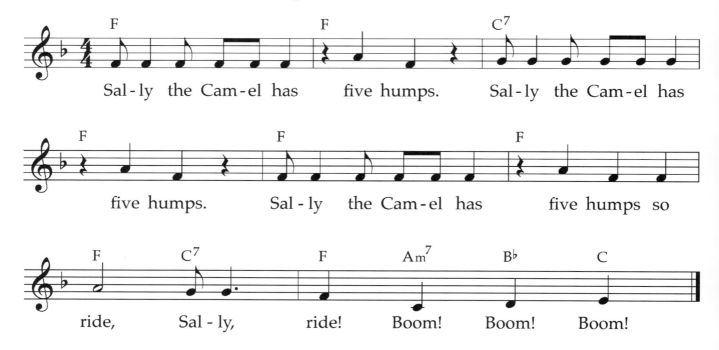

Sal-ly the Cam-el has five humps. Sal-ly the Cam-el has

five humps. Sal-ly the Cam-el has five humps so

ride, Sal-ly, ride! Boom! Boom! Boom!

2nd Verse
Sally the camel has four humps.
Sally the camel has four humps.
Sally the camel has four humps,
So ride, Sally, ride!
Boom! Boom! Boom!

3rd Verse
Sally the camel has three humps.
Sally the camel has three humps.
Sally the camel has three humps,
So ride, Sally, ride!
Boom! Boom! Boom!

4th Verse
Sally the camel has two humps.
Sally the camel has two humps.
Sally the camel has two humps,
So ride, Sally, ride!
Boom! Boom! Boom!

5th Verse
Sally the camel has one hump.
Sally the camel has one hump.
Sally the camel has one hump,
So ride, Sally, ride!
Boom! Boom! Boom!

6th Verse
Sally the camel has no humps.
Sally the camel has no humps.
Sally the camel has no humps,
'Cause Sally is a horse, of course!

Soup, Soup

Soup,   soup,   we   all   like   soup.   Tip   your   bowl   and   drain   it,

let   your   whis-kers   strain   it.   Hark!   Hark!   The   fun-ny   noise,

list - en   to   the   gurg   -   ling   boys.

I'm a Little Piece of Tin

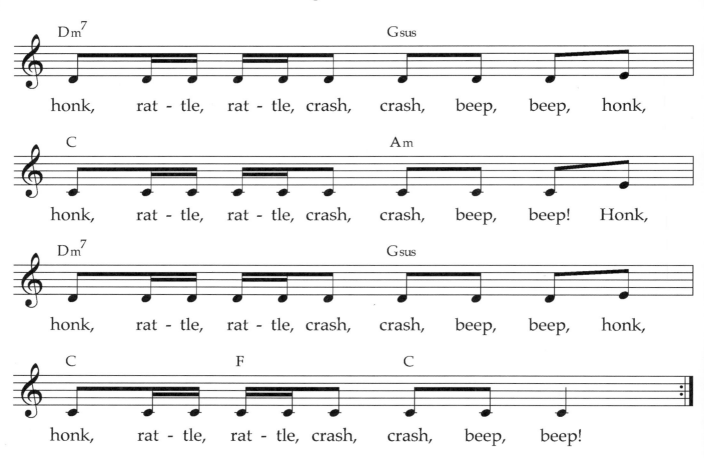

Sheet Music and Lyrics Index